SELECTIVE MUTISM

AN ASSESSMENT AND INTERVENTION GUIDE FOR THERAPISTS, EDUCATORS & PARENTS

BY AIMEE KOTRBA, PHD

Published by
PESI Publishing & Media
PESI, Inc
3839 White Ave
Eau Claire, WI 54703

Cover Design: Amy Rubenzer
Layout: Bookmasters
Editing: Marrietta Whittelsey

Printed in the United States of America

ISBN: 978-1-55957-006-0

PESI
Publishing
& Media
www.pesipublishing.com

TABLE OF CONTENTS

ACKNOWLEDGEMENTS

I have decided that only crazy people write books while working, owning a business, and raising a family. And only crazier people support them in that pursuit. To my husband, Jeff—you are the craziest. Thank you so much for your support, your love, and your encouragement through this writing process. Thank you to my kids; they are too young to know what Mommy is doing when madly typing on her computer, but they give me laughter and happiness that energizes me to keep trying when I feel like giving up. None of this would be possible without my parents; you always told me that I was capable of doing anything, and although you aren't really right (have you seen my golf game?) you made me believe in myself. I love you both. A big thank-you to Michael Rustman, Ed.D., Connie Kotrba, and Lisa Kovac, Ed.S., BCBA for editing, cleaning, and generally making this book sound better than it otherwise would have. I want to express my gratitude to the board members of the Selective Mutism Group, past and present. I am inspired by your commitment to children with selective mutism and their families. Finally, a thank you to those who work with me at Thriving Minds Behavioral Health—Marla Fields, Sheri Mehlhorn, and Katelyn Reed, M.S.—for your support and for sharing in my excitement. I have been blessed to work with you.

INTRODUCTION

When my publisher asked that I write an introduction explaining why I wrote a book on selective mutism, my first reaction was to pen a few paragraphs that could basically be boiled down to, "I am writing in order to help people" (such a psychologist answer). However, when I really thought about *why* I decided to write a book about selective mutism, I realized that it was out of pure frustration. Frustration at the lack of research-based information on selective mutism that is available to professionals and parents. Frustration about the myths that still exist in the general public concerning selective mutism. Frustration when other psychologists tell families that selective mutism can't be treated. Frustration when people unknowingly use terms like "Jake refused to talk to me," as if the child is making a malicious decision not to speak. Frustration that we haven't adequately spread the word about selective mutism.

I wrote this book out of that frustration, to assure you that selective mutism is treatable, as well as to provide a toolkit in your work. This book is for schools, professionals, and parents who are looking for realistic and helpful strategies that can be implemented in the school, clinician's office, and public to increase speech and decrease anxiety. Children with selective mutism *can* be effectively treated, and this book will give you step-by-step, clear, understandable instructions on how to help. I am regularly contacted by therapists and parents who exclaim with great surprise (and pleasure) that after implementing these strategies, their child made abundant strides in both confidence and verbalizations. I want to impart that same hope to you.

I also want to impart a good work ethic—this will not be easy. Mark Twain once said, "Habit is habit, and not to be flung out of the window by any man, but coaxed down-stairs one step at a time." Children with selective mutism stopped speaking due to extreme anxiety, but the lack of speech quickly becomes a habit, and this habit can take time—and a lot of hard work—to change. But have no doubt—the outcome will be worth it. Being able to speak to peers, participate in class, and interact with people in public restores a child's confidence and broadens his or her future prospects. By working through this book diligently and with patience, *you* can help a child thrive.

CHAPTER 1

MORE THAN JUST SHY?

- Jamie sits quietly on her own, while the other students laugh and talk around her. When Jamie is asked a question, peers say dismissively, "she doesn't talk." The teacher, sensing her discomfort, skips her during circle time. Her parents stop trying to put her in extracurricular activities when it becomes clear she is distressed.

- Sam squirms in his chair, panic building in his seven year old body. He is unable to tell his teacher either verbally or nonverbally that he has to use the bathroom. Suddenly, children start staring as Sam has an accident in his seat.

- Ashley's anxiety fills her with dread when she enters the music room. Unable to utter a sound, she withdraws and stares. Her teacher, convinced that Ashley is not trying, gives her a zero. She fails the course.

- While playing on the playground, Morgan falls off the monkey bars and breaks her wrist. She is terrified and in pain, but cannot tell anyone she is hurt until the end of the day—five long, painful hours later when she returns home.

These upsetting stories are just a sampling of what children with selective mutism can experience. Children with selective mutism often have difficulty completing normal childhood tasks: telling a teacher about an injury, relating socially to other children, making a request to use the bathroom, asking a question in class, or participating in a group project. Their plight too often goes unaddressed and untreated, because the disability is not well known or understood. Parents and school personnel may know that these behaviors have moved outside the realm of "normal behavior" and that intervention is necessary, but often do not know what steps to take.

What can parents do to help their child feel more confident? If the child does not speak, how can the school assess the child's knowledge? How does the school identify a plan of action? How do parents advocate for their child when they do not understand what is wrong? There are many questions and far too few answers.

Research has demonstrated repeatedly that early intervention is imperative in successfully treating selective mutism (Bergman, 2013). Early intervention helps avoid issues that arise from a continued lack of communication, participation, and socialization. Each day that the child avoids talking deepens his or her struggles, which can lead to increased anxiety, decreased self-esteem, and more difficulty in changing the behavior pattern. For the child's sake, parents and professionals must intervene early and effectively.

These stories can be frightening and upsetting, especially for parents or caregivers of children with selective mutism. The good news is this: with the right treatment, these scenarios can be avoided. Selective mutism is treatable, and children treated with effective interventions tend to have wonderful outcomes. Children with selective mutism can learn to be brave, advocate for their needs, ask questions, respond to peers and adults, and speak with confidence. Nothing feels better than observing a child who never spoke in class raise their hand to proudly answer a question or perform in the school musical. I have sat with parents, grandparents, and teachers as they cried tears of joy watching a child with selective mutism succeed. This book will provide research-based, concrete techniques to help children slowly face and overcome their fears, increase confidence, and increase speech. Implementing the ideas found in this book will make a difference in the life of a child with selective mutism.

This book is not intended to provide all of the answers or give a cookie-cutter approach to the treatment of selective mutism, but to provide parents, school personnel, and treating professionals with guidance, ideas, worksheets, and activities that will assist in the effective assessment and treatment of selective mutism (SM). The treatment of SM is like a dance, with each participant reacting to the moves of their "partner," and therefore it has to be individualized to each child and each specific presentation of symptoms. However, a basic treatment overview can give clarity in a world muddled with misinformation and lack of specifics about selective mutism.

WHAT IS SELECTIVE MUTISM?

Selective mutism is an anxiety disorder, characterized by a lack of verbal (and sometimes nonverbal) communication in specific settings. Although these children can speak well in certain environments (e.g., at home with family or good friends), they are mute or extremely hesitant to communicate in other social settings (e.g., school, restaurants, stores). It is important to note that these children are able to use and understand speech, but demonstrate a persistent inability to communicate in specific settings, and this inability becomes a pattern of behavior. In order to diagnose selective mutism, the mutism must be ongoing for at least one month. However, it is important to note that a lack of verbal communication in the first few months of the first year of school (whether that is preschool or kindergarten) is considered within normal limits. To be diagnosed, the student must present impairment in daily functioning (typically at school or in public settings) for more than a month, and other explanations for the lack of verbal communication (such as a speech impairment, autism, and stuttering) must be ruled out. Children can have co-occurring diagnoses (such as autism, speech impairments, etc.) but these other diagnoses cannot better explain the lack of speech in the school and/or public environments.

DIAGNOSTIC CRITERIA FOR SELECTIVE MUTISM (DSM-5 CODE 313.23)

- Consistent failure to speak in social situations, such as school or in public, despite speaking in the home or in comfortable settings.
- The lack of speech has educational or social implications.
- The mutism lasts at least one month (or six months if in the first year of school).

• The mutism is not better accounted for by a communication disorder or a pervasive developmental disorder (such as Autism). This does not mean that a child can't have cooccurring diagnoses, such as selective mutism and a communication disorder, but the other diagnosis can't account entirely for the mutism. (American Psychiatric Association, 2013)

As with all emotional impairments, there is a continuum of severity, from children with mild impairments to children with very severe symptoms. Children on the mild end of the spectrum may be able to speak to certain individuals, but remain mute with others. They may be able to respond when a direct question is asked of them, albeit in a quiet voice with fleeting eye contact, but struggle to initiate verbally. Children with a more severe presentation may be unable to speak to anyone in a school setting or a public place; they may even have difficulty talking to extended or immediate family members whom they see often. Some children at the more severe end of the continuum may even have difficulty responding and/or initiating communication *nonverbally* (i.e., nodding, pointing, writing) while participating in the classroom setting and doing schoolwork.

Research suggests that SM impacts approximately 1 in every 100 children in elementary school (Bergman, 2002). Although 1% of the elementary school population may sound quite rare, it is similar to the current prevalence rates of autism, a diagnosis that is widely known and recognized (Blumberg, 2013). Some researchers believe that prevalence rates may actually be higher, because a lack of knowledge about the diagnosis or a lack of concern about the symptoms may be masking a much higher incidence. Since children with selective mutism generally are not a behavioral problem (instead, they tend to be quite compliant, studious, and intelligent), the lack of verbal communication may not be enough for parents and school personnel to seek out treatment. Parents may not be aware that a problem even exists, since these children are usually quite talkative and outgoing at home. Even if parents are aware that the child is not talking in school, they themselves may have a history of social anxiety and may downplay the significance of the symptoms (e.g., "I did not talk until third grade either—he is just shy"). Schools may hesitate to intervene or provide special education services if there is no overt academic need. In addition, pediatricians are not always familiar with the specifics of selective mutism. Because they see *many* temperamentally anxious or shy children who refuse to speak in well-child visits, a mute child doesn't raise a red flag and referrals for treatment are not made (Schwartz, 2006).

Research supports an alarming lag between the onset of symptoms and the start of treatment for children with selective mutism. Age of onset for selective mutism is approximately 2.7 to 4.1 years of age. A *problem* with verbal communication or anxiety (although rarely a specific diagnosis) is usually first identified when the child enrolls in school—typically at age 5 to 6 years old. The main reason that lack of communication becomes an issue in school is the difficulty in evaluating the child's reading or learning levels when they can't communicate. Research typically demonstrates a one-to-three-year lag between symptom onset and/or the identification of an issue (e.g., mutism in the school setting) and the appropriate diagnosis and start of treatment. Thus, the average age at which the child is formally referred for an assessment or treatment may range from 6.5 to 9 years of age. For some children this equates to four school years of avoiding speech before intervention begins. This lag in diagnosis and treatment is particularly concerning, as selective mutism becomes increasingly less responsive to treatment over time.

Selective mutism has been found in numerous prevalence studies to be more common in females than males—girls are almost twice as likely to be diagnosed with SM (Kumpulainen, 2002, Garcia, 2004). Two main hypotheses exist for this difference. First, it may be a true gender difference—internalizing disorders such as anxiety and depression seem to be more common in females (with externalizing disorders diagnosed more commonly in males). Since SM is an anxiety-based disorder, it is possible that it occurs more frequently in girls. Second, it could be a lack of appropriate diagnosis in males. Our society tends to have higher expectations of verbal socializing in young girls than boys. Consider how young boys socialize. They play and bond through shared activities, such as sports, video games, and pretend physical play. There are fewer demands for conversations during these activities. In contrast, young girls socialize and relate to peers through speech—telling secrets, role playing, and interacting with dolls. Thus, when females do not communicate, it may stand out to adults in a much more significant manner. As a result, the girls with SM may be judged as more impaired socially and academically.

Although each child is different, there are some common traits of children with selective mutism:

- difficulty responding and initiating verbally
- difficulty communicating nonverbally
- generally average to above-average intelligence
- perceptive and sensitive
- freezing and/or awkward body movements when anxious, such as stiffness, tense shoulders, strained facial expressions, etc.
- poor eye contact
- slowness to respond (a long latency between the question and the child's response).

It is rare that selective mutism occurs independently of other fears and anxiety issues. Commonly co-occurring disorders include social phobia and generalized anxiety disorder. Additionally, children may experience speech and language issues, school refusal/anxiety, and other types of anxiety disorders (such as obsessive-compulsive disorder or specific fears such as dogs, insects, and storms), specific hearing impairments, and defiance. Children with selective mutism frequently have anxiety about using the toilet in public places (due to the fear of asking teachers to use the restroom, and/or the loud, sudden sound of an automatic toilet flushing, the fear of being "stuck" in a social situation with other peers in the restroom, and/or the "performance anxiety" of others hearing them use the toilet). Thus, they may have more urinary accidents (daytime enuresis).

Communication Issues in Selective Mutism

Selective mutism co-occurs frequently with communication delays, disorders, or weaknesses. Although research provides differing prevalence rates (depending on the speech and language issues being examined), most studies suggest that approximately 30-75% of children with selective mutism also have communication deficits (Klein, 2012). These communication weaknesses can be very subtle, and parents and/or caregivers may not even be aware of them as an issue. Weaknesses can be any impairment in the ability to understand or formulate language, and may include:

- pragmatics (the ability to use language to socialize, including greeting people, starting and maintaining conversations, and using facial expressions and eye contact)
- voice (abnormal pitch, quality, and/or loudness)
- fluency (fluid and efficient word-finding)
- articulation (formulating clear and distinct speech sounds)
- grammar (using correct sentence structure)
- semantics (appropriate word selection).

When children are effectively evaluated for speech and/or language deficits, the most striking deficits appear to be in the areas of oral narration and complex expressive language tasks. Researchers have found that parents may be the most skillful evaluators of their child's speech and language issues (when highly trained to give the evaluation). Even when parents evaluated the child in the home setting, 42% of children in a recent study exhibited expressive language deficits at or below the 5th percentile for their age (Klein, 2012).

There are no specific answers as to why children with selective mutism have higher rates of these communication deficits. It could be:

1. Independent of selective mutism—a coincidental presentation of both issues in one child.

2. A precursor to the development of selective mutism—children recognize to some degree that speech is not fluent, clear, or easy to develop, and this causes them discomfort or anxiety. In order to avoid the anxiety and negative feedback they might receive for speech that is difficult to understand or "wrong," they become mute.

3. Aggravating the selective mutism—both occur as a coincidence, but the communication deficits cause the mutism symptoms to be much worse than would otherwise be the case.

4. Lack of communication experience—children with SM do not participate in as much practice communicating verbally and therefore do not receive as much corrective feedback pertaining to their fluency and grammar.

Recent research hypothesizes that some children with SM (possibly as many as 75% of children with selective mutism) may also have subtle differences in hearing and processing that can negatively impact their ability to talk (Muchnik, 2013). When humans vocalize, the auditory system needs to prevent over-stimulation by its own vocalizations. In layman's terms, the brain masks the sound of the speaker's voice when they are talking. This masking allows the speaker to hear, process, and understand external sounds while vocalizing. For instance, if I am talking and someone interrupts and talks at the same time, not only can I hear them over the sound of my own voice but I can also process what they are saying. Research hypothesizes that this part of the auditory system (the middle-ear acoustic reflex, or MEAR) is functioning abnormally in a subset of children with selective mutism, and children with these abnormalities may struggle to process auditory information that comes in as they are speaking. This abnormality posits several interesting outcomes. First, a child who is already anxious and fearful of saying or doing the "wrong" thing, may discontinue speaking in social or academic situations so as to not miss important auditory information. In effect, they "face the dilemma of consciously or subconsciously choosing between speaking or listening" (Muchnik, 2013). This reduced speech would be particularly expected in situations that require a lot of auditory processing and where social anxiety may already elicit an anxious response (e.g., classroom settings or conversations with peers). Furthermore, many children with SM describe their voices as "weird" or "strange"; if they are hearing an "unmasked," amplified version of their voice in their own head, it may very well sound strange and aversive to them.

Bilingual children have much higher rates of SM, and higher rates of SM exist in communities with many ethnic minorities or immigrant families (Krysanski, 2003). These children tend to have pre-existing anxiety or social inhibition, and may become mute because of the uncomfortable feelings surrounding using an unfamiliar language. Consider this scenario: a young girl moves from Brazil to the United States at the start of her kindergarten year. Her native language is Portuguese, and this is the primary language spoken at home by her parents and sister. Her parents note that she has a history of separation anxiety and has always disliked being the center of attention. When she starts school, she sees other children speaking the English language well and feels frustrated and embarrassed that she cannot clearly communicate. She stops speaking in order to avoid the embarrassment of making a mistake or saying something incorrectly, and this pattern of not speaking is solidified as time passes, even though she is learning the new language at an appropriate pace. She becomes known by classmates as "the kid that doesn't talk" and fears that if she does talk at some point, peers will laugh at her accent or get overly excited about hearing her voice, bringing unwanted attention. The longer this behavior continues, the more difficult it is to change. Unfortunately, this avoidant behavior can transfer back to the native language, and the child can become mute even in the language they feel most comfortable speaking. This transference of mutism may be because as the child becomes very good at avoiding communication, the avoidance generalizes to all communication.

It is important to note two things—first, being bilingual does *not* cause selective mutism. In fact, there are many benefits to bilingualism, and parents should not feel guilty after the fact for teaching their child a second language. Second, there is a normal silent period when learning a new language; therefore, mutism for a few weeks to up to six months is considered within the realm of "typical" for those learning a second language. It is notable that the younger the child, the longer the silent period may last. Older children may be silent for a few weeks to a few months, while younger children may be relatively silent for a year while learning a new language (American Speech-Language-Hearing Association). However, if signs of mutism are spilling over into the native language, the child seems quite temperamentally anxious in other areas, or they are not beginning to speak their new language aloud after six months to a year, assessment for selective mutism may be warranted.

How Do You Differentiate Social Phobia and Selective Mutism?

Social phobia and selective mutism are often confused due to their many similarities. In fact, approximately 70-100% of children with SM receive an additional diagnosis of social phobia (Yeganeh, 2003). Both SM and social phobia are effectively treated with the same or very similar psychopharmacological treatment and cognitive behavioral therapy with the goal of decreasing anxiety and increasing social activities. Both can involve a distinct fear of interacting. Family history studies support a genetic relationship between selective mutism and social phobia: 70% of first degree relatives of children with SM have social phobia, and 37% have selective mutism (Chavira, 2007). Researchers continue to explore the differentiation between the symptoms and etiology of selective mutism versus social phobia.

Social phobia is diagnosed when the child has a persistent fear (such as the fear of being humiliated, embarrassed, and/or scrutinized) of one or more social and/or performance situations where they are exposed to unfamiliar people (both peers and adults). When exposed to these situations, the child becomes anxious. Due to the anxiety, these children either avoid these situations or endure them with intense anxiety and distress. These symptoms must last for at least six months and interfere with school and/or socialization significantly. Selective mutism also has an avoidance component and anxiety, which is where the symptom overlap lies.

Some clinicians and researchers hypothesize that selective mutism is an extreme expression of social phobia. As a result, in the fifth edition of the *Diagnostic and Statistical Manual of Mental Disorders* (DSM-5), selective mutism was subsumed under social anxiety as a severe childhood manifestation of social anxiety (American Psychiatric Association, 2013). Researchers are still examining the evidence behind this theory and are currently obtaining mixed results. Many children with SM enjoy social interactions that are nonverbal (e.g., do not have an expectation of speech) and do not avoid them; they specifically avoid verbalizations. Children with social phobia, however, tend to avoid all types of social interactions. While the onset of selective mutism is approximately three to five years of age, Social phobia typically manifests between the ages of eleven and thirteen. Furthermore, if SM was simply a severe presentation of social phobia, we would expect that the children with SM would rate themselves as having more anxiety than children with social phobia. When children with SM were compared in a controlled research setting with children with social phobia, children with SM *did not* rate themselves as experiencing higher levels of social distress than the children with social phobia (Yeganeh, 2003). Two reasons have emerged as to why there may be a discrepancy between the level of anxiety that *others* perceive in SM and the level of anxiety the children self-report. First, it may be that children with SM have found a successful avoidance strategy—they lower their anxiety by refusing to speak. Second, adults could be over-interpreting the child's anxiety—they assume that a child who does not speak must be overcome with fear. More research is needed to delineate the relationship between selective mutism and social phobia.

WHERE DOES SELECTIVE MUTISM ORIGINATE?

As with most anxiety disorders, there appears to be a genetic component in the development of selective mutism. The genetic predisposition for anxiety that runs in families can manifest differently for different family members, but the core genetic component appears to be the same. Thus, family members may have other types of anxiety (e.g., social phobia, generalized anxiety disorder, obsessive compulsive disorder) but the genetic makeup of the child results in the anxiety manifesting as selective mutism. It is not uncommon for children with selective mutism to have parents with characteristics of SM or social phobia, and their siblings are more likely to exhibit symptoms of selective mutism (particularly identical twins).

In addition to a genetic predisposition to anxiety, research demonstrates some abnormalities in brain reactivity in children with selective mutism. Most research into the brain mechanisms of anxiety find that the amygdala plays a large role in modulating our reaction to and perception of anxiety (Davis, 1992). When our brain perceives a situation, person, or event to be dangerous, our amygdala reacts with the fight or flight response, sending out signals from our cortex to physically and mentally prepare our body. However, if the perceived situation is not truly dangerous, our cortex has a very difficult time "turning off" the signal from the amygdala. This is the way in which reactions to "irrational" or minor dangers develop into physiological anxiety responses. Likewise, research has shown over-reactivity in the amygdala of children with selective mutism, meaning that they may perceive situations that have a verbal component as being extremely threatening. Furthermore, they have a much more difficult time returning to baseline functioning in comparison to non-anxious peers, and thus their brain functioning appears hyper-vigilant and over-reactive across time. This lack of habituation, or return to baseline, may be why these children's fear is persistent and difficult to reduce.

As noted before, often parents of children with SM also have social anxieties, and this can affect the parent's ability to cope with their own anxiety around their children. Resultantly, children may be not only genetically predisposed to anxiety, but may also be learning anxious behaviors via parental modeling. Parents may avoid social situations secondary to their own anxiety, reducing the child's exposure to novel situations and people and limiting the number of opportunities the child has for practicing "brave talking." Additionally, parents may inadvertently portray the world and unknown people as dangerous, unpredictable, and untrustworthy, thereby increasing the child's anxiety.

For example, I met Jenny's parents at a diagnostic intake session (the first session before treatment, where a background history is obtained and a plan for treatment is developed). It was obvious that Jenny's mother, Allysa, was uncomfortable in my office—she did not make eye contact, spoke softly, and took several deep breaths during the meeting. During our discussion, Allysa admitted that Jenny had seen her mother have several panic attacks in the past, and although the panic attacks were now well-controlled with medication, she still struggled with social anxiety. Allysa reported avoiding large crowds, evading phone calls (Jenny's father handled much of the "public relations" for the family), and staying in the home most of the time. Because of her mother's anxiety, Jenny's family rarely went out for dinner at local restaurants, and the children were not involved in any extracurricular activities. When I inquired about Jenny's speech with family friends or extended family, her mother admitted that they do not really have many friends and do not see extended family. The children were not allowed to play with neighborhood kids, since the parents viewed the families as "questionable" and "rough."

Unfortunately, Jenny has experienced a nature/nurture double whammy. Not only is there an obvious predisposition to anxiety in the family history, but this anxiety is modeled overtly and conveyed through subtle parenting decisions on a daily basis. Additionally, Jenny's parents delayed treatment because of the anxiety around seeking out a referral and making an appointment with a professional they did not know. For a parent who has social phobia, calling the office of an unknown professional, making an appointment, talking to them about intimate details of the family life, and allowing that person to interact with their child may be more than they can handle.

THE HISTORY OF SELECTIVE MUTISM

Originally named "*aphasia voluntaria*" by German physician, Adolph Kussmaul, in 1877, selective mutism was thought to be caused by a traumatic episode in the child's past or by inadequate and/or abusive parental relationships with the child. Kussmaul and subsequent practitioners believed that the lack of communication in some settings while being able to speak in other settings was a voluntary decision (Kussmaul, 1877). In 1934, Swiss psychiatrist Moritz Tramer changed the name to "elective mutism," continuing to underscore the belief that the child was "electing" not to speak. The name was finally changed to selective mutism in 1994, consistent with current research that the mutism occurs in select situations because of the *anxiety experienced in those environments as opposed to a decision to withhold speech* (Sharoni, 2012). Confusion still occurs with the name selective mutism, as some laypeople believe that the child can "select" when they will and will not speak, leading to beliefs that the driving force of the disorder is oppositionality, control, and manipulation. That is not the case—these children are literally unable to speak in certain "select" environments. The term selective mutism emphasizes that the anxiety concerning speech is selectively dependent on the social context.

Originally, selective mutism was thought to be caused by a traumatic incident in early childhood, such as neglect, abuse, or being witness to violence. The hypothesis proposed that these children, who experienced such trauma, had chosen to become mute to keep a family secret or punish the offender. Treatment focused on uncovering the traumatic episode and addressing the underlying feelings or improving family relationships. However, no research has found a causal link between the development of selective mutism and traumatic past experiences.

In her book "*I Know Why the Caged Bird Sings—After Six Years of Mutism*," Maya Angelou tells the story of a traumatic childhood and her subsequent mutism for six years following a horrific experience. This infrequently occurring mutism is *not* selective mutism; instead, it can be a symptom of post-traumatic stress disorder (PTSD). Children with mutism as a result of PTSD generally have a normal developmental background, where parents observed them speaking to others and saw little significant anxiety until immediately after the traumatic experience. This sudden loss of speech tends to be relatively short-lived and is not associated with a shy, anxious temperament prior to the trauma. In contrast, children with selective mutism have a history of anxiety about talking to others in public, such as in preschool, church, or daycare; the mutism does not appear spontaneously.

Progression of Mutism

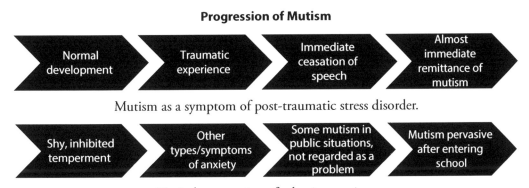

Mutism as a symptom of post-traumatic stress disorder.

Typical progression of selective mutism.

Although we have no evidence that SM develops because of a traumatic episode, many children have experienced some form of trauma prior to the development of their selective mutism, generally related to being forced to unwillingly face their fear of speaking. When teachers, strangers, extended family members, and others do not understand SM, they may believe that the child is being noncompliant and attempt to "force" them to speak or withhold things like use of the bathroom, lunch, or privileges to motivate them to talk. This "flooding" of anxiety may be a distressing experience for some children.

Traumatizing or distressing interactions as a result of selective mutism can occur in many ways. For example, a third grade boy with selective mutism may have an understanding teacher, but the lunch monitor does not know about the diagnosis or his challenges with using his voice. When the child gets to the front of the lunch line, the monitor asks him what he would like to have for lunch, and instead of answering he looks down and smiles. His lack of response, coupled with the smile, is misread by the lunch monitor as a smirk, and given the long line behind him she becomes frustrated. "Unless you can tell me what you want, I cannot serve you. Sit down and let me know when you are ready to order; you are holding up the line." How many days will go by until that child eats? He probably will not be able to order, particularly in front of a long line of peers, and asserting himself to seek out his teacher to get help is also incredibly anxiety-provoking. He may have to wait until an adult notices he is not eating and determines the cause—and that could be quite a few hunger-filled days or weeks later. Sounds pretty traumatic to me.

For children with selective mutism, the avoidance of speaking in select situations and environments acts as *deliberate self-protection* from the intense anxiety experienced by the child, *not deliberate oppositionality* (Bergman RL, 2002). Too commonly, adults in the lives of children with selective mutism begin to believe that the child is just being "difficult" or "rude." The natural reaction to this interpretation is increasing the communication expectations for the child and then punishing, shaming, or disciplining him or her for not speaking. Unfortunately, these consequences may both increase the anxiety around speaking and lead to lowered self-esteem and self-efficacy.

IS IT REALLY ANXIETY, OR JUST CONTROL?

Occasionally at a school meeting or when speaking to extended family members, an adult will make a comment such as, "It seems to me Lisa chooses not to speak when adults are around. I think that she is just trying to get out of doing what she is supposed to do. She will speak to her best friend when I am in the room, but when I get close she puts her hand over her mouth and stops talking. I just do not see the anxiety at all." Parents receive school report cards with notes like, "Shannon refused to participate in group activities" or, "Brendan chose not to do his oral presentation today; instead, he ran out of the room when he was called to the front of the class." The anxiety that these children experience is so debilitating that they often describe it as feeling like " I cannot get the words out of my throat" or, "I will die if I get up in front of the class!" My challenge to adults who believe the child is simply being controlling is to take a full day and make it a goal not to speak outside your home. That means no asking where the bathroom is in public, no ordering at restaurants, and no talking to friends. No answering the phone. When people say something to you at the store, look down and do not respond.

Don't get hurt, lost, or confused, because you are on your own; you cannot ask for assistance. Is this a fun day? Is it enjoyable to remain silent, or just exhausting and anxiety-provoking? It is difficult to believe that a child, simply out of spite, defiance, or manipulation, is able to stay silent day after day, year after year, particularly when many of these kids miss out on enjoyable experiences, friendships, and even rewards because they are unable to speak to others.

I have experienced a similar feeling when traveling in foreign countries. I know in certain environments that speaking will not be successful because no one will understand English, and I do not speak the native language. This is incredibly anxiety-provoking for me—what if I need to use the bathroom and do not know where it is located? What if I get hurt and need medical intervention? What if I am lost and need directions? This is the everyday plight of a child with selective mutism.

Children appear to have two different reactions when it comes to the expression of anxiety, and these reactions likely originate from our natural fight-or-flight response to fearful stimuli. When placed in situations we perceive as dangerous, our bodies react by preparing us to either fight, freeze, or flee (avoid). If the fear is real (e.g., an impending car accident or a large bear), this physical preparation is helpful—it causes our muscles to tense, our heart rate to accelerate, our breathing to quicken, and our thoughts to move rapidly. Even if our life is not in danger, and the physical preparation is not justified, our amygdala may be slow to quiet the "danger signal" and we still tend to act with aggression or avoidance. The majority of children with selective mutism react with avoidance when feeling anxious, but a minority group of children, when pushed too quickly to communicate, may react with "fighting" (oppositional) behaviors.

In practical terms, many of the children I see in the clinical setting look outwardly anxious. They freeze when approached, demonstrate poor eye contact, slip into occasional tearfulness, and avoid verbal (and at times nonverbal) communication. Less frequently, a child will present as anxious/oppositional; they look angry and may grunt or lash out physically. At times, they may even have a sly smile on their face and slowly shake their head when I encourage them to take part in learning "brave behaviors." For example, a patient I began seeing at age seven was completely unable to talk to me for the first several sessions but, if she felt at all prompted to communicate, would scream loudly, kick, hit, and hide under the desk. I scheduled her as the last session of the day so that she did not frighten other patients in the clinic with her loud screams. Despite outward appearances, her mutism was not born of defiance, but instead the defiant behaviors (strong-will, temper tantrums, and physical aggression) were the expression of the extreme anxiety she was experiencing. She was a "fighter" instead of a "fleer." It is possible for children to have co-occurring oppositional behavior, just as many children in the general population can be defiant at times. In fact, research suggests that rates of oppositional behavior in children with SM in both home and school mimic rates in the general population. The mutism is not a symptom of the oppositional behavior. It is a symptom of the anxiety.

THREE SUBSETS OF SELECTIVE MUTISM

New research suggests that there are three different subsets, or classifications, of children with selective mutism (Cohan, 2008). The first group, exclusively "anxious" children with selective mutism, demonstrate freezing behavior, difficulty with both nonverbal and verbal responding and initiating, and significant social anxiety. In initial research, this group appears to be the smallest subset, and they may have the lowest levels of symptom severity. This reduced severity may be a product of the lack of complications such speech/language delays.

The second class, "anxious/oppositional," is portrayed by defiant behaviors specifically when prompted to speak or engage. This defiance may be exhibited through running, active avoidance, stubbornness, and/or controlling behavior. It is unclear if this behavior is independent of the selective mutism or a result of the anxiety (and subsequent avoidance) stemming from the fear of communicating.

The final class, "anxious/communication-delayed," exhibit mild to severe communication delays along with clinically significant social anxiety. These children may have expressive and/or receptive language delays. In research, they score higher than the exclusively anxious group in symptom severity and behavioral issues, suggesting that overall this group may be the most severely impaired, and therefore the most complex to treat (Cohan, 2008).

Thus, a full conceptualization of the developmental weaknesses related to selective mutism could look like the following:

Developmental Conceptualization of Selective Mutism

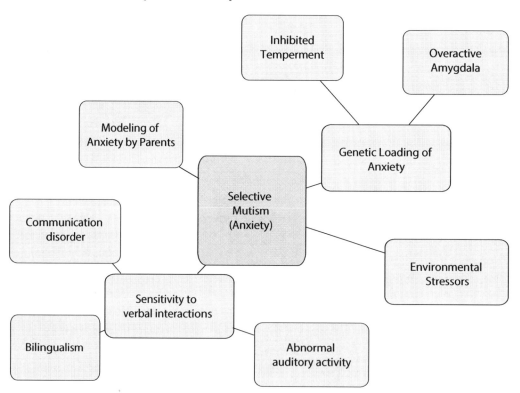

How Do I Know This Is Selective Mutism, and Not Just Shyness?

It is extremely common for children to be hesitant, quiet, and tentative when faced with new and unknown situations and people. For example, if a child is sent to a new school or day camp, we as adults would find it completely within the realm of "normal" for that child to remain quiet for a day or two while he or she adjusted to the new situation and new people.

Shy children are typically very observant, taking in all of the new information, processing it, getting their bearings, and slowly opening up. They may be slow to warm up, speak, make eye contact, or engage in activities provided. However, with time they would begin engaging and communicating with peers or adults at a slow, steady pace. These children are typically known as introverted or "slow-to-warm-up." Introversion is generally considered to be a personality characteristic, resulting in similar behavior in most environments.

A child with selective mutism presents in a different manner. While these children may also be hesitant or inhibited at first, they may eventually engage in a group setting without speaking. They may tell parents that they "love" school, and teachers report that they seem to be enjoying themselves and playing with peers. Some children with selective mutism may not even appear outwardly anxious. However, despite the seeming comfort, there tends to be a consistent pattern of inability to speak in these situations, either to peers, adults, or both. Although the child is interacting well, participating and looking outwardly relaxed, speech does not eventually follow as it would with a "shy" child. Even after the warming-up stage has passed, the child is still unable to speak. The shy child acts in a similar hesitant and inhibited manner across situations, while the child with selective mutism almost appears to have two different personalities—the silent, anxious, inhibited child in certain public situations and the outgoing, charismatic, talkative, moody, and even bossy child when comfortable. Parents frequently discuss with me the frustration of these dual personality characteristics, since the world does not get the opportunity to see their child as they "really are"—fun, outgoing, silly, and smart.

Use of the DSM-5 criteria can also be helpful in distinguishing shyness from selective mutism. Children with temperamental shyness or inhibition would not meet the criteria listed above, and thus their characteristics would be considered within the realm of normal behavior.

If It Is More Than Shyness . . . Should We Seek Treatment?

The average time period between the observation of an "issue" (e.g., the school letting parents know that the child is not speaking in the classroom) and starting treatment (whether that is intervention in the school, parents helping the child practice being brave, or seeking out treatment with a mental health professional) can be months or even years. Some children never actually receive help for their selective mutism. Many factors may lead to this delay in appropriate diagnosis and intervention. Frequently, parents receive advice from others such as: "Don't worry; she is just shy" or "She will grow out of it." Still others will tell stories of their own slowness to speak in school ("I did not talk in school until third grade and I am fine"). It can be quite difficult to find treating professionals with knowledge or expertise in selective mutism. As a result, families wait for the child to mature and begin speaking over time or as they feel more comfortable only to realize weeks, months, or years later that no progress is really being made.

Another delaying factor can be that selective mutism is occasionally misdiagnosed as an autism spectrum disorder. Since some of the symptoms of SM mimic the characteristics of autism (e.g., poor eye contact, blank facial expression, awkward/stiff body postures, a lack of speech), it is easy to see why a misdiagnosis could occur. It is notable that when a child with selective mutism presents with autism-like symptoms, these symptoms present only in select settings (specifically when the child is uncomfortable or anxious). This differs from children with primary autism spectrum disorders, who exhibit these behaviors across all settings. See Chapter 3 for a more detailed discussion on differential diagnoses.

Finally, after evaluations have ascertained a diagnosis of SM, many professionals and schools are not sure how to effectively treat selective mutism. There is a plethora of misinformation in the public realm about selective mutism, including the tendency to blame parents or assume that there is a horrible trauma in the past. At a recent workshop, a speech-language pathologist told me a story about her daughter's experience as a camp counselor. Her daughter had a child in her cabin that, she explained to her mother, had been sexually abused by her father. Her mother, the speech-language pathologist, was aghast to hear this news—she knew the family and would never have predicted that the father would be involved in child abuse. Concerned, she probed further and her daughter explained that the child had selective mutism, and therefore the camp staff assumed that the child's father must have abused her. Her comment was, "that is what causes selective mutism, right?" This tendency to blame parents or the environment may inhibit parents from seeking help for fear of being blamed or unfairly scrutinized. Other misinformation suggests that taking away all prompts and opportunities to verbalize will allow the child to become comfortable (which will, in turn, lead directly to an increase in talking). As there are few experts in selective mutism and few opportunities for training in the intervention, many adults elect to forgo intervention out of fear that misguided treatments may cause harm.

CHAPTER 2

SILENCE AS A SAFETY NET

BEHAVIORISM 101

In order to understand the conceptualization of selective mutism, it is necessary to think of behavior in terms of reinforcement and punishment. All behavior is subject to reinforcement (which increases future behavior under similar conditions) and punishment or lack of subsequent

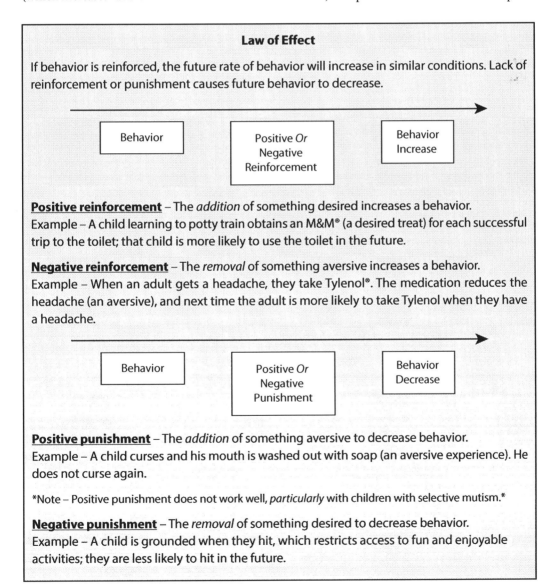

Law of Effect

If behavior is reinforced, the future rate of behavior will increase in similar conditions. Lack of reinforcement or punishment causes future behavior to decrease.

| Behavior | Positive *Or* Negative Reinforcement | Behavior Increase |

Positive reinforcement – The *addition* of something desired increases a behavior.
Example – A child learning to potty train obtains an M&M® (a desired treat) for each successful trip to the toilet; that child is more likely to use the toilet in the future.

Negative reinforcement – The *removal* of something aversive increases a behavior.
Example – When an adult gets a headache, they take Tylenol®. The medication reduces the headache (an aversive), and next time the adult is more likely to take Tylenol when they have a headache.

| Behavior | Positive *Or* Negative Punishment | Behavior Decrease |

Positive punishment – The *addition* of something aversive to decrease behavior.
Example – A child curses and his mouth is washed out with soap (an aversive experience). He does not curse again.

*Note – Positive punishment does not work well, *particularly* with children with selective mutism.*

Negative punishment – The *removal* of something desired to decrease behavior.
Example – A child is grounded when they hit, which restricts access to fun and enjoyable activities; they are less likely to hit in the future.

reinforcement (which decreases future behavior). Children (and adults) carry out behaviors for a reason. In the vast majority of circumstances, we do not continue a behavior that gives us nothing in return; that is just too much of a waste of time and effort. Instead, we engage in behaviors because there is a reinforcing outcome, or we continue with behaviors because when we do, something negative is taken away. In short—we do things either to get something or to avoid something.

A good example of utilizing positive reinforcement is a household chores chart. If we wanted to increase the likelihood that a child would consistently make his bed, we could provide positive reinforcement, such as praise (verbal reinforcement) or candy/stickers/prizes (tangible rewards) when he made his bed. The effective reward always depends on the child—some children will work hard for a little sticker, while others demand larger tangible prizes or privileges for rewards. Another option would be negative reinforcement, or taking away something perceived to be aversive or undesirable to increase the behavior of making his bed. We could take away another disliked chore contingent on his making his bed (e.g., "If you make your bed, you do not have to do the dishes."). In general, reinforcement works more quickly and effectively for learning in comparison to punishment . . . and it is more enjoyable for everyone.

CONCEPTUALIZING SELECTIVE MUTISM

Selective mutism is understood as a pattern of avoidance of anxiety-provoking situations, accidentally strengthened through negative reinforcement.

Behavioral Conceptualization of Selective Mutism

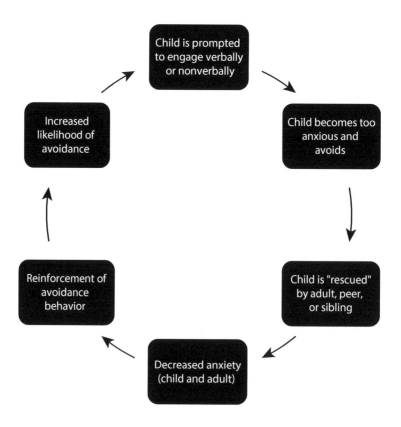

The cycle begins with a child who likely has a genetic loading for anxiety and perhaps biological tendencies to become very over-aroused and anxious when in situations where communication is demanded. The child may also have a language delay, auditory processing weakness, or other commonly co-occurring complication. The child is then exposed to expectations for communication (e.g., a question from a teacher). The child attempts to avoid the communication or interaction (top of the diagram). Avoidance is a natural reaction to anxiety (think of the fight-or-flight response to anxiety—the child is fleeing from the expectation to speak). When the child avoids the interaction, it is socially uncomfortable for others to wait for a response and someone generally jumps in to "rescue" or speak for the child. This could be a teacher, parent, peer, or sibling. When the expectation for communication is suddenly removed, the child (and the others involved in the interaction) feels much better; anxiety and discomfort is removed (bottom of the diagram). This reduction of anxiety accidentally reinforces the behavior, and so the next time the child is in a similar situation, they are more likely to avoid verbal communication.

Referencing the information on reinforcement versus punishment above, we can see that this is an example of negative reinforcement—the action of taking away aversive or noxious stimuli (anxiety) when someone rescues the child negatively reinforces the child's avoidant behavior. Others around the child learn through reinforcement, too, and are more likely to quickly jump in and "rescue" the child by speaking for them or reducing expectations for communication. This "rescuing" may take the form of speaking for the child or reducing the number of direct questions or prompts for speech given. Peers may begin to state, "Johnny doesn't talk" before the child even has an opportunity to respond.

We hypothesize that the beginnings of this pattern of behavior are entirely driven by anxiety—the child becomes too anxious and does not speak. However, over time the behavior of avoiding speech may be motivated less by overwhelming anxiety and may function more as a learned avoidance mechanism. Thus, the child experiences less anxiety as he becomes more skilled at avoiding verbal communication.

Consider a real-life example. A child is at the store with her mother. They are approached by another adult, who compliments the child on her outfit. Both the parent and the adult turn to the child, expecting her (as is socially appropriate) to say, "thank you." Instead, what do we see with a child with selective mutism? She likely hides her face, steps behind her mother, and is silent. At this point, someone rescues the child from that awkward silence—either the mother says, "thank you" for the child, or the adult may say something like, "Oh, I see she is just shy." The child now is relieved of the expectation to talk, and the mother and other adult are relieved of the socially uncomfortable silence and obvious anxiety of the child. All are negatively reinforced (by the removal of the aversive anxious feeling), and the pattern of behavior continues.

It is important that parents and other adults are not considered at fault for their "rescuing" behavior. No right-minded parent or adult enjoys watching a child squirm in anxious situations, and understandably it is our general response to attempt to make situations less anxiety-provoking for children whenever possible. This occurs out of caring and empathy for the child. We become quite good at stepping in and "saving" the child from the anxiety—at some point we as adults also learn to avoid altogether what causes the child anxiety. We stop asking the child questions, pass over them in circle time, and do not place them in group projects with peers. We complete tasks for the child, communicate for them (this is *extremely* common), rearrange a setting to accommodate the lack of speech, and allow whispers and nonverbal communication to take the place of speaking. Soon, not only is the child avoiding the anxiety—so are the adults around them. This becomes a concerning situation—the child has no reason or opportunity to become verbal. While the likelihood of a child with selective mutism answering a question or participating verbally may be small, if there are no opportunities given by adults to participate or verbalize, the chance of the child with SM asserting themselves and speaking is absolutely zero.

As this pattern of behavior continues (i.e., the child avoids, someone steps in and saves, avoidance is reinforced by reduced anxiety for all involved), both adults and peers become very practiced and successful in rescuing roles. Imagine how frequently this pattern of behavior occurs. How many times per day are you prompted to speak, including answering questions, talking on the phone, initiating to others, requesting information, or maintaining a conversation? It might be hundreds of times per day. If we are conservative, we could hypothesize that a typical child is engaged verbally approximately 100 times per day. That is 700 opportunities to practice this behavioral pattern each week, 3,000 opportunities per month, and 36,500 practice opportunities each year. If you practiced anything that frequently, you would get quite good at it, and it would come naturally. The children engaging in this behavioral pattern obtain plenty of practice avoiding and therefore develop compensatory behaviors, such as getting needs met through nonverbal communication, miming, or whisper buddies (i.e., friends who tell others what the child wants or needs). Adults receive plenty of practice speaking and answering for the child and saving them from anxiety-provoking situations. This tendency to save the child from the anxiety is not a result of disordered family dynamics or parental pathology. It is a natural response from those who care about the child. While it is out of love and care that adults and peers protect the child from anxiety, this also accidentally causes those same anxieties to persist and even worsen with time.

As noted before, some individuals view the avoidance of speaking as defiance, control, or manipulation. Children with SM may not look particularly anxious because they are successfully avoiding an anxiety-provoking interaction; occasionally the child may even appear defiant to an observer. Although the symptoms may look like defiance, the avoidance related to selective mutism is a naturally occurring reaction to anxiety, not unlike other phobias. For example, I have to admit that I have an intense fear of roller coasters. This fear has only become more poignant as I have aged and my stomach is not as strong as it used to be. When I am in the vicinity of roller coasters, my fight or flight mechanism kicks in, and I do everything in my power to avoid riding them. My husband would literally have to take me kicking and screaming to the line. I would look VERY defiant and oppositional if I was asked to directly face my biggest fear by riding a roller-coaster. I do not generally look anxious to the passerby on a normal day, as I am rarely near roller coasters (I have developed quite a well-practiced avoidance pattern). My seeming oppositionality in that scenario is not born of a defiant personality—it is the result of my avoidant reaction to anxiety. Such is the occasionally oppositional reaction to speaking of kids with SM.

IMPACT ON PARENTS, SIBLINGS, PEERS, AND SCHOOL PERSONNEL

In my office, parents most commonly discuss concerns about their child's anxiety and how they wish there was a way for their child to "let go, enjoy life, and be themselves." If they are truly honest, many parents admit feelings of anger, frustration, confusion, and embarrassment, particularly concerning their child's behavior in public. They do not know how to respond when the child cannot answer a polite stranger who compliments them. They get (generally unwanted) advice from well-meaning family members about parenting skills and the need to just "be tough" with the child, thereby forcing them to talk. Most importantly, parents often do not know how to help their child practice being brave.

Interestingly, polite words are often the hardest words for children with SM to say, and this adds to the embarrassment of parents. Hi, goodbye, sorry, please, thank you, and excuse me are incredibly difficult and prompting the child to say these words almost always leads to immediate avoidance. This may be because of the extensive practice of avoidance of polite phrases—these are the words all parents prompt their child to say on a regular basis, and therefore these kids have garnered much practice avoiding these prompts. Furthermore, children with selective mutism may fear that using these words with others opens the door to a conversation or increased interactions. I often encourage parents not to prompt their child to say these words any longer when starting treatment. We can make them a focus or a goal at a later date.

Siblings are impacted by SM as well. At times, more than one sibling may exhibit characteristics of SM (particularly identical twins). This makes sense, since we know that anxiety has a genetic predisposition and one sibling may be modeling avoidance for the others. Alternatively, siblings may begin to talk for the child with selective mutism, answering questions and developing a particularly outgoing and assertive personality to make up for their sister's or brother's quiet nature. They may even step in and "rescue" the child from scenarios where there is a prompt to speak.

Peers are usually quite socially accepting of children with SM in younger grades and will continue to play and interact even when the child with SM does not respond verbally to them. However, as children age, the characteristics of SM (i.e., difficulty responding and initiating verbally and nonverbally, possible social anxiety, an inability to play a role in group projects, etc.) begin to alienate children with SM from their peers. The number of their friendships may begin to decrease as friendships evolve from interactive play to a relationship cultivated by communication and joint understanding. As they age, peers become less understanding of the individual with SM and begin to exclude them from activities. If left untreated, children with SM in later years have a higher likelihood of eventually becoming social outcasts—the kid in class who no one really remembers, socializes with, or invites to activities.

Teachers and school personnel frequently have reactions similar to those of parents—they vacillate between a concern for what the child is experiencing, a fear of "breaking" or "ruining" them through an anxiety-provoking experience, and frustration, anger, and confusion as to how to help. Selective mutism can be particularly perplexing for teachers when they are held responsible for assessing the child's knowledge and involving the child in classroom activities. Furthermore, many teachers admit to natural feelings of hurt when the child does not talk to them. It is easy to take it personally when a child with SM cannot talk to you, but it may have absolutely nothing to do with you and/or your personality. There seem to be unspoken "rules" concerning who children with SM talk to, in what environment, and under what circumstances. Many times, the children themselves cannot explain or identify these "rules," but they are apparent in the child's behavior. They may talk to friends at soccer, but not at school. They may talk to mom and dad while walking up to the school grounds, but after stepping onto the sidewalk they stop responding verbally. Some children will talk to certain teachers but not others. There seems to be very little rhyme or reason to these "rules" and boundaries, and they can be frustrating to peers and teachers alike. Friends may become hurt when the child with SM stops speaking to them suddenly when they move to a different environment. The kindest teacher in the school may feel upset when the child cannot talk to her, but will talk to the gruff, grumpy janitor. We must understand that there are factors that we are not aware of, *and that the child is not aware of,* that are influencing their ability to talk. It is not the fault of the child or the potential communication partner, but just a manifestation of the anxiety the child feels that we do not fully comprehend.

IMPLICATIONS OF THE AVOIDANCE PATTERN

The continued avoidance of speech in public scenarios has long-lasting academic, social, and behavioral outcomes. Children with SM tend to be well-behaved and are generally not disruptive even when unable to participate in class. However, teachers in today's schools are trained to engage students in activities such as team-learning projects, oral presentations, partner reading, and group discussion. Classes promote not only listening but also speaking, reading, and participation, the bases of language comprehension and production. Thus, there are numerous long-lasting academic implications for kids with SM who are unable to participate in these educational skill-building activities. First, they are difficult to assess or test, particularly in reading. Because of the lack of speech, teachers and other school personnel may be unable to evaluate the child's understanding of a concept, resulting in decreased opportunities to give corrective feedback. Second, the children may be unable to participate in group projects or activities. Many problem-solving techniques, including learning to compromise and work effectively with others, are learned within the context of group projects. Third, the children do not have the opportunity to practice oral presentations, show-and-tell, or public speaking. Finally, the children do not have the ability to ask a question or clarify information if they do not understand. For example, consider how math builds consistently on past knowledge. If a child does not understand a specific mathematical skill and is unable to ask for help or request that the teacher explain further, that child will likely fall behind in later math concepts. As the child struggles to demonstrate the knowledge they are acquiring, a gap opens between abilities and achievements (Sharoni, 2012).

In addition to academic implications, there are many social implications for children with SM. There are not higher rates of bullying concerning these children, but there may be difficulty making and keeping friends. Children with selective mutism, as they age, simply begin to fade into the social background. Even in early elementary school, kids with SM are treated differently. They may be treated as if they are younger or less capable than they really are by peers (who have the wonderful intention of "helping" them but accidentally reduce expectations and their opportunities to be verbal). Some are popular, but classmates assume a protective role and, despite the peers' good intentions, this protection accidentally preserves the problem. The child with SM frequently becomes known as "the kid that doesn't talk."

Finally, there are behavioral implications in public and in extracurricular activities. Children with SM may be restricted in their participation in extracurricular activities if these activities have verbal demands that can't be met by the child. More frightening is the thought that children with selective mutism cannot cry out for help if they are in danger or alert an adult if they are hurt or in trouble. One of my patients fell into a ditch on the way home from school. She injured her leg and ankle and could not escape from the ditch because it was too high to climb out. Because she was unable to cry out for help, she lay there for several hours before a search team found her. If she had been able to speak, she would have been heard almost immediately as there were several people within shouting distance.

If left untreated, there are many possible negative outcomes as the SM progresses (Steinhausen, 2005). The child is at a much higher risk for later generalized anxiety disorder, specific phobias, and major depressive disorder. They have a higher incidence of refusing to attend school and poor school performance as they become older. In adulthood, they are more likely to self-medicate with alcohol and marijuana and more likely to choose careers that do not demand frequent socialization. Since selective mutism is considered a disorder of childhood, adults with these symptoms may be diagnosed with severe social anxiety or avoidant personality disorder. These serious implications demonstrate the need for early intervention. If we intervene early and effectively, we can avoid the negative impact on the child and those around him/her.

Unfortunately, attempting to obtain early intervention can be confusing and misinformation is prevalent. Some of the literature and websites on selective mutism recommend that adults do not try to encourage the child to talk at all—that when all pressure is removed, the child will spontaneously begin speaking. Research does not support this premise that a total lack of intervention leads to verbalizations. It also does not make sense in the framework of conceptualizing selective mutism as a type of phobia. If you avoid any interaction with the object or event causing you anxiety, do you suddenly become brave and no longer frightened? No.

Consider the following example. Joey is afraid of dogs; because of his fear, Joey's family and friends organize his daily life to avoid dogs altogether. The family stops going to houses of friends who have dogs. They throw away all books and videos featuring dogs. They even stop going on walks because of the potential of seeing a dog. Will Joey suddenly stop being afraid of dogs and decide they are wonderful pets? Will he say to his parents, "that fear of dogs was silly? I love dogs now"? Of course not. In fact, his fear may become more ingrained because he has not had any opportunity to experience dogs as non-threatening. The idea of dogs as dangerous will remain fixed.

In order to address and reduce his fear of dogs, his friends and family would need to slowly and gently introduce him to dogs that are safe, during which time he could begin to develop a different conceptualization of dogs. Instead of all dogs being seen as threatening, Joey would begin to see that some dogs are safe for interaction. Approaching a child's fear this way helps them gain practice in facing their fears at a reasonable pace. In much the same way, if we remove all exposure to communication and all intervention encouraging the child to speak, it is extremely unlikely that they will suddenly talk.

Using the "wait and see" approach with children who have selective mutism can be very detrimental because of the way selective mutism develops—through a continuous pattern of avoiding communication. An approach that is inactive and allows that pattern to continue occurring only strengthens the pattern of avoidance. Therefore, *each day that goes by in which the child does not work to practice new "brave behaviors" and instead continues the practice of avoidance is not neutral.* Allowing the pattern of avoidance to continue makes it increasingly difficult to break.

Imagine being known as "the kid who doesn't talk." How challenging would it be to just start talking? Others will likely overreact to your first words, an outcome which kids with SM dread. "You talk. Say it again, say it again." Intervening early saves children from being defined by this persona—"the child who doesn't talk"—and reduces the response of others when they eventually communicate. Early intervention also assists in developing self-efficacy—the feeling that they are capable of being brave, making changes in their behavior, and reaching goals. Most of the children with SM describe a desire to talk; if we help them do so, they experience clear feelings of success. In a recent session, a first grader with SM and I were chatting, and in passing I asked her why she thought it was so easy to talk to me in my office but hard to talk to people in school. "Because you make me talk." she replied with a smile. Chuckling, I asked her if perhaps everyone at school should "make" her talk. "Yes, I wish they would." she responded. She desperately wants to talk to others, but simply cannot get the words out.

We as parents, teachers, school professionals, and mental health professionals want children to be successful and happy. Children with untreated selective mutism are likely not reaching this potential. We MUST intervene early to provide the best future outcomes.

CHAPTER 3

ASSESSING FOR SELECTIVE MUTISM

It may appear that a diagnosis of selective mutism is easy to make: If a child talks at home and does not talk at school or in public, they probably have selective mutism. The process of substantiating a diagnosis, sifting through related issues, and determining the best course of action can be much more complex. Like any psychological diagnosis, consideration of selective mutism involves researching the child and the family. However, unlike other diagnoses that may not take into consideration environmental factors, the diagnosis of selective mutism necessitates a thorough investigation of the child's school and public life. Assessing for selective mutism (and ruling out other disorders) is a four-step process:

1. Diagnostic interview with parents/teacher/caregivers

2. Questionnaires

3. Observation of the child in different environments and in the presence of different individuals

4. Rule out related or co-occurring disorders or weaknesses

DIAGNOSTIC INTERVIEW

A diagnostic interview is the first and most important piece of evidence in making a case for selective mutism. First, the clinician must determine the exact circumstances of the current behavior (not speaking). Through interviews with parents, teachers, and caregivers, the following information, in detail, must be obtained:

**Who** **does the child currently talk to?** Who are they unable to talk to (e.g., who are the people regularly in their lives with whom they cannot yet verbally communicate)? Who are they most likely or most interested in communicating with and who are they least likely or interested in communicating with?

**What** **incentivizes the child to communicate, or in what circumstances would they be most likely to talk? If they need something?** If someone asks them a direct question? If they are interacting one-on-one with an adult? If approached by a peer? It is likely that there are particular activities in which the child is more likely to talk (e.g., while engaged in a fun play activity as opposed to answering a question in front of the class).

**Where** **is the child able to speak?** Only at home? In public to parents if no one is watching or listening? On the playground, but not in the classroom?

**How** **does the child communicate?** Gestures? Writing? Sounds? Whispering? Short responses?

The more detail obtained during the interview, the more specific the treatment plan will be. For example, it would be a waste of time and energy to focus treatment on something the child is already easily able to do, such as responding to the parent in a store. Relatedly, we may not expect the child to speak immediately to the teacher's assistant if the child has never done so before. For an example of a diagnostic interview, see page 107. Please note that the diagnostic interview is best conducted as an interactive, in-person interview, and not given as a questionnaire for parents to complete independently. This will allow the interviewer to follow up in obtaining more detail about the child's modes of communicating.

QUESTIONNAIRES AND RATING SCALES

Following a complete diagnostic interview, questionnaires and rating scales can compare children to "typically developing peers" in the realm of selective mutism symptoms as well as related anxiety symptoms. There is currently only one published questionnaire specific to selective mutism—the Selective Mutism Questionnaire (Bergman, 2008). The Selective Mutism Questionnaire (SMQ) was developed to obtain information about the child's communication across three main settings—home, school, and public. The SMQ is a 17-item parent report questionnaire normed for children ages 3-11. Parents are asked to rate their child's frequency of speech in several different settings and with different possible conversational partners. Parents rate the frequency of each item using a 4-point scale (3 = always, 2 = often, 1= seldom, 0 = never for speaking situations); thus, overall lower scores indicate less speech. Scores are then compared to a "clinical" group of children with selective mutism, as well as "typically developing" children to determine if speech production is within normal limits or if it is significantly discriminate from "typically developing peers." The SMQ demonstrates high reliability in consistently identifying children who have selective mutism, without detecting children who have other forms of anxiety disorders.

The SMQ can be used in two ways—quantitatively and qualitatively. Quantitatively, the SMQ can be used to provide scores, as noted above, as evidence of a possible selective mutism diagnosis. Alternatively, it also can be used qualitatively in conjunction with Dr. Elisa Shipon-Blum's Selective Mutism-Stages of Communication Comfort Scale© (SM-SCCS) to describe the severity of the selective mutism and build goals for school. The SM-SCCS is a guide to determining the child's current stage of communication. See page 113 for the four stages of social communication.

In order to use the SM-SCCS qualitatively, users can look for the general trend in scores within each subsection. For instance, if parents scored mostly 0's for their child's speech in social situations, that child could be said to be functioning at Stage 0 in public settings. If most scores were 1's in the school setting, the child could be said to be functioning generally in Stage 1 in the school setting. Using the SMQ and SM-SCCS in this way not only allows professionals and parents to describe the child's current speech, but also provides descriptive verbiage for goal setting in special education plans (e.g., "Child will move from Stage 1 to Stage 3 with teacher in a one-on-one setting," "Child will move from Stage 0 to Stage 1 in the general classroom setting," etc.). More information on special education evaluation and planning will be provided in Chapter 7.

In addition to the SMQ and SM-SCCS, other anxiety-specific or general mental health questionnaires can be given to the child, parents, and teachers. One of the restrictions on using additional measures for children with selective mutism is age norms; most children diagnosed with selective mutism are quite young (younger than 8 years old), but many overall anxiety questionnaires are normed for children ages 8 and up. Some appropriate questionnaires include:

- The Screen for Childhood Anxiety Related Emotional Disorders (SCARED). The SCARED provides both a self-report and parent-report form measuring symptoms of childhood anxiety disorders, including separation anxiety, social anxiety, generalized anxiety disorder, obsessive-compulsive disorder, panic disorder, traumatic stress disorder, and specific phobias. It is normed for children ages 8 to18.
- The Social Phobia and Anxiety Inventory for Children (SPAI-C). The SPAI-C requires a third grade reading level, and allows the child to self-report on a range of potentially anxiety-provoking social situations. It is normed for children ages 8 to14 (Beidel, 1996).
- The KID-SCID (childhood disorders version of the Structured Clinical Interview for DSM-IV) is a structured interview with questions related to mood, anxiety, and disruptive behavior disorders for children ages 7-17 (Matzner, 1997).
- Multidimensional Anxiety Scale for Children (MASC). The MASC is used to assess major anxiety symptoms including physical symptoms of anxiety, social anxiety, separation anxiety, and panic disorder. It is normed for children ages 8-19 years (Pearson Education).
- Behavioral Assessment System for Children (BASC). The BASC is a behavioral rating scale and self-report personality scale which measures internalizing and externalizing symptoms as well as adaptive skills. It includes a self-report, parent-report, and teacher-report, and is normed for ages 4-18 (Reynolds, 2004).

DIRECT STRUCTURED OBSERVATION

Prior to designing treatment, many questions need to be answered: what verbal communication needs to be shaped, which people and environments need to be introduced, which reinforcements are most helpful and most likely to be easily employed in the home and classroom, and what accidental reinforcement is being provided from teachers, peers, parents, siblings, and friends. While interviews and questionnaires can garner helpful data, direct observations can provide a wealth of information. In fact, behavioral observations have been described as the "key lynchpin" of assessment and treatment of selective mutism (Kearney, 2006). In order to help plan treatment, the clinician should engage the child in a structured observation. It is beneficial, if possible, to do an observation in three main settings:

1. At home
   a. A videotape made by parents of the child when they are comfortable, relaxed, and verbal.
   b. An interaction with the clinician in the home setting (i.e., the clinician visits the child's home to learn more about the family dynamic and play with the child in the environment where they likely feel the most comfortable).
2. In the school
   a. The clinician sits quietly and discretely in the classroom, watching the group factors that may influence the child's speech or lack of speech (see the information on functional behavioral analysis below).

3. In a novel location (such as a psychologist's office, a restaurant, or a store)—a sample structured observation sheet is included on page 114.

   a. The clinician observes the child one-on-one with the parent in a novel setting, such as an office playroom.

   b. The clinician observes the outcome of introducing a novel adult or child into the interaction.

   c. The novel person prompts the child with questions, increasing in difficulty level (from yes/no questions to forced choice questions and ending with open-ended questions).

   d. The novel person exits the room, and the clinician observes the child as they return to baseline.

If the child does not already know the clinician, the first observation should be in the classroom. This would allow the clinician to observe the child without awareness that he is the focus of the observation. As a psychologist, I perform the public observation in my office. In my office, there is a playroom with a one-way mirror and a sound system that allows me to watch the interactions between parents and children in a play situation. However, even if there is no access to a one-way mirror, an effective observation could be done with a webcam in the room. Finally, an observation could be made by an examiner sitting in the same room as unobtrusively as possible (with the expectation that their presence may change the behavior of the child; therefore, this is not a preferable way of conducting an observation if any other mode is possible).

STRUCTURED SCHOOL OBSERVATION

The process of conducting a structured school observation can provide an enormous amount of data and information to the assessment of selective mutism (Schill, 1996). In order to provide information for treatment planning, an observation would take into consideration the same questions asked in the diagnostic intake: who does the child talk to, where does the child talk, and how does he or she communicate? The clinician can code communicative behaviors (e.g., gestures, whispering, mouthing, sounds, one-word responses, multiple-word responses, longer utterances, or initiating). Additionally, it is helpful to note to whom the child directs communication (e.g., known adult vs. novel adult, known peer vs. novel peer). The clinician should track where the child communicates (e.g., one-on-one, in a small group, in front of a larger group). Finally, it is important to record key antecedents (e.g., demands/expectations of the situation or lack thereof), outcomes or consequences of the mutism, and possible reinforcers used to produce speech. Generally, the function of the mutism is predicted to be avoidance-based. A sample school observation sheet is included on page 116.

Information garnered through the direct structured observation and classroom observation can be used to determine what intervention technique is recommended. In Chapter 4, these data will be considered in determining whether to use *shaping* or *fading* techniques in treatment.

It is important to note that the child with selective mutism may surprise you by speaking to you in the evaluation, particularly if the evaluation occurs in a one-on-one private setting. Kurtz (2011) reported that when evaluating students with SM following a brief rapport-building interaction, 27% of the children responded to the examiner's first question, 36% responded to the second question, and 43% responded to the third question asked by the examiner. This should not necessarily rule out selective mutism, but should be noted for consideration when determining the best intervention.

RULING OUT CO-OCCURRING DISORDERS

As discussed in the previous chapters, there are many different disorders that can occur in conjunction with selective mutism, including other anxiety disorders and speech/language weaknesses or disorders. There are also many diagnoses that may share symptoms with selective mutism, such as autism spectrum disorders. The main differential symptom between selective mutism and other anxiety disorders, developmental disorders, or language-based disorders is that the child with selective mutism *can* talk in certain situations, but is not able to use that same quality/consistency/volume of speech in other situations due to anxiety. Thus, a child could have an autism spectrum disorder and selective mutism, if they are able to speak in one situation (despite the quality or social appropriateness of that speech) and not in a more public environment. The characteristic differentiating autism from selective mutism is the clear gap between the child's behaviors in a "safe" or comfortable environment, such as in the home setting, and behavior in social or performance settings, such as the school environment. In order to evaluate for these other disorders, a full psycho-educational evaluation could also include (but is not limited to):

- speech/language evaluation
- evaluation of intellectual functioning (a multi-dimensional nonverbal intelligence scale, such as the Leiter-R may be most appropriate)
- educational evaluation
- hearing evaluation
- oral-motor examination of coordination and strength in the muscles of the jaw, tongue and lips
- evaluation for autism symptoms (such as the Autism Diagnostic Observation Schedule). Please note that many of the scoring criteria of the ADOS rely on communication with the examiner, and the child with selective mutism may not be able to communicate consistently either verbally or nonverbally. Thus, the ADOS should only be used as one piece of data in an evaluation for autism.

MAKING A DIAGNOSIS

Who can make a diagnosis? For an official diagnosis, the determination must be made by a clinical psychologist, licensed clinical mental health counselor, clinical social worker, psychiatric nurse, speech/language pathologist, or physician (such as a pediatrician or psychiatrist). However, many other individuals are also very important in both the evaluation and treatment team. One of the most important and helpful professionals is the speech/language pathologist.

Speech/language pathologists (SLP) can receive a lot of contradictory messages on their role in the evaluation and treatment of selective mutism. At times, they are encouraged to be involved, but in other situations they may be told that selective mutism is an anxiety disorder and should therefore be addressed by professionals who have expertise in anxiety. They themselves may be uncomfortable with the idea of being involved in the treatment of an anxiety disorder. Is selective mutism an anxiety disorder? Yes. Is selective mutism a pragmatic communication disorder? Yes. Social interactions are the basis for language learning, and children with reduced social interactions may have fewer opportunities for language learning, feedback, and practice. Therefore, having an SLP on the evaluation and treatment team can be extremely helpful.

The role of the SLP in the evaluation team is obvious—ruling out fundamental communication disorders and describing symptoms, situations, and weaknesses that may impact the child's ability to use speech consistently and correctly. As noted before, if the child has an underlying communication problem, he or she is at a higher risk for selective mutism and can have a longer treatment timeline. The American Speech Language Hearing Association lists multiple roles and responsibilities for the SLP, including assessing and treating the social aspects of communication, or social pragmatics. These can and should be included in the evaluation of a child with selective mutism, and should be considered when making a diagnosis.

A speech and language assessment of a child with selective mutism might include:

- Speech production
- Fluency (the rhythm of speech)
- Receptive language (what the child understands)
- Expressive language (what the child can convey verbally, including word-finding, sentence formulation, narrative quality, etc.)
- Pragmatic language (knowledge of the social rules of speech)
- Articulation (how speech sounds are made)

With this information, an SLP can determine if the child's speech and language skills limit him/her socially, if they are using language appropriately, and if there are sufficient opportunities to communicate. Possible treatment targets may include motor planning and articulation, syntax and morphology, increasing sentence length and complexity, addressing word-finding weaknesses, sentence formation, and teaching/rehearsing pragmatics of speech.

Children with selective mutism can be quite a challenge to evaluate in a reliable, valid manner. Their difficulty responding both verbally and nonverbally, slowness to response or inefficiency working quickly, and avoidance of interacting with novel adults can easily lead to much lower scores on tests and, without consideration of the impact of anxiety, a misinterpretation of the child's ability level. Additionally, anxiety can mask a child's language abilities (Klein, 2012). We as practitioners must be very careful in the interpretation of our test results, as it is unfair to a child if we take the scores we receive as their overall level of potential.

Recently at a presentation for SLPs, I was discussing the tendency for scores to be an under-estimate of the child's ability, both cognitively and academically, when one of the participants raised her hand to share an experience. She had been working with a child diagnosed with selective mutism who had been referred to the school psychologist for a cognitive evaluation. When the evaluation team met to review the testing results, the psychologist provided his diagnosis of cognitive impairment, based on extremely low scores in intelligence testing. This was not the child the SLP knew—the child appeared quite intelligent, and his teachers reported that he always did well on written work. When asked to provide more information on the testing, the psychologist admitted that the child "chose not to respond" and therefore received a zero score on most items, resulting in an IQ score in the severely impaired range. This circumstance resulted in an invalid interpretation of scores. Thus, it is important to be cognizant of the effect of selective mutism on all testing, and to be sensitive to the resulting outcomes.

Professionals (both speech/language pathologists and psychologists) can increase the validity of evaluation outcomes for children with selective mutism by using a few "alternative" assessment strategies:

- First, the assessor should attempt to develop a relationship with the child, as opposed to jumping directly into testing. Prior to the evaluation, the evaluator may consider having 2-3 sessions with the child in a fun, play-based interaction without the expectation for speech.

- The evaluation should be completed either one-on-one with the evaluator or with only the child, parent, and evaluator in the room. Some children are able to speak to or read to their parent with another individual in the room listening.

- The assessor should take care not to engage the child in unnecessary eye-contact, as sustained eye-contact from unfamiliar people can make children with selective mutism uncomfortable (Shipon-Blum, 2003). That does not mean no eye-contact, but that the examiner should "busy herself" when possible with other activities and limit direct eye gaze.

- Parents may be used as test presenters. In fact, research has shown that parents trained in test presentations can be effective evaluators and can produce significantly higher language test scores in comparison to professionals (Klein, 2012).

- Evaluators may have to use more non-specific and qualitative evaluations of speech through videotapes or audiotapes of the children in comfortable situations.

When the evaluator has data suggesting a pattern of speaking comfortably in at least one environment versus a lack of speech in more public environments, and other reasons for this difficulty in speaking have been ruled out through a diagnostic interview, clinical observation, psycho-educational evaluation (including speech, hearing, and differential diagnosis consideration), we can feel confident in diagnosing selective mutism. And luckily, this evaluation plan provides a wealth of great information to prepare for the next step—treatment.

CHAPTER 4

RE-WRITING THE AVOIDANCE SCRIPT

Following the evaluation and diagnosis of selective mutism, we begin the fun (but admittedly challenging) step—the intervention. The main sections of intervention discussed in this chapter include:

1. Determining the intervention "team" and main interventionists
2. Building rapport between the child and interventionists
3. Educating the child about his/her anxiety
4. Developing the behavioral treatment plan, including a communication ladder (shaping) and stimulus fading plan

This chapter is arguably the most practical, as it provides the "meat" of the intervention. Please consider making notes in the margins and filling in the workbook sections as you proceed.

DETERMINING THE INTERVENTION "TEAM" AND MAIN INTERVENTIONISTS

In Chapter 2, the conceptualization of selective mutism identified avoidance as a coping strategy. The child becomes overwhelmed with anxiety and tries to avoid the interaction or occurrence which is causing the anxiety. An important piece of the intervention involves what often happens next—individuals accidentally step in and rescue the child. This behavior is born of the desire to comfort the child and reduce the anxiety, but can backfire when adults, peers, parents, teachers, and siblings help the child maintain the avoidance behavior. There are many ways that "rescuing" occurs:

- Parents respond for the child (e.g., order for the child at restaurants, answer for the child, tell extended family members what the child wants, etc.)
- Teachers stop asking the child questions in class
- Peers stop interacting verbally with the child in class
- Peers or siblings quickly state, "Jamie does not talk." or answer for the child when others ask a question
- Others provide the child with easy nonverbal communication tools (e.g., only ask yes/no questions to allow head shaking/nodding, accept and encourage written responses, etc.)

To begin building the intervention team, it is important to begin thinking about those individuals in the child's life who accidentally rescue and reinforce the avoidance. Who may be "accidental reinforcers" in the child's life, and what do they do to help maintain the avoidance of speech?

Person	How do they inadvertently reinforce avoidance?

These accidental reinforcers are those individuals that we particularly need on the treatment "team"—we need them to become knowledgeable about selective mutism and learn ways to stop reinforcing the avoidance. A "team" in the general sense of the word (which broadly encapsulates those who know the child's strengths/weaknesses and are armed with some strategies to assist in building "brave" skills) may include:

- Parents
- Teachers
- School administrators
- Speech/language pathologists
- Social workers
- School psychologists
- School counselors
- Behavioral analyst/behavioral specialist
- Clinical psychologists
- Classroom peers/friends
- Siblings
- Extended family, particularly common caregivers

However, a core treatment team (those responsible for carrying out the actual intervention) includes the parents, the keyworker within the school setting, and the mental health professional outside of the school setting (e.g., behavioral analyst, clinical psychologist). All members have different responsibilities:

A *keyworker* is the individual inside the school setting who is responsible for:

1. Managing and implementing the behavioral intervention inside the school setting
2. Generalizing speech to all school environments and with as many people as possible
3. Communicating with the teacher, parents, and treating psychologist

Most frequently, a keyworker is a person with either a mental health or speech/language background and training, such as a school psychologist, behavioral analyst, social worker, counselor, or speech/language pathologist. However, determining a keyworker who can regularly meet with the child is difficult—professionals are overworked, caseloads are at capacity, and schools may have a limited number of special education personnel. Therefore, the functional or realistic criteria for a keyworker are someone who can consistently work with the child, is caring and interested in the intervention, is willing to be flexible and learn more about selective mutism, and is a good personality match for the child. I have been on treatment teams where the keyworker was a principal, school nurse, teaching assistant, paraprofessional, and reading specialist, among others. The teacher is not recommended as a keyworker. This is not because of training, ability level, or desire, but simply because teachers usually have 30+ children regularly in their care and finding time to focus one-on-one regularly with a specific child may put too much stress on an already stressful job. It is usually preferable that another individual take the position of the keyworker but communicate very closely with the teacher.

Another important characteristic of a keyworker is availability for consistent intervention. Today's schools encourage group pull-outs for special education services. This likely will not work for the child with selective mutism—at least not at first. Although there are some notable exceptions (such as children who speak more easily when they are in the room with a friend or sibling), in order for most children to be successful, they need to first meet with the keyworker in one-on-one interactions on a frequent basis. In order to make consistent and significant progress, meeting individually with the child for 15 minutes three times per week is the minimum necessary. There is a good reason for this, these children are practicing using avoidance strategies every single day, many times per day. In order to change their behavioral repertoire, we need to practice brave behaviors many times per day. The more frequent the practices, the better. If practices occur fewer than three times per week, it is very hard to get traction and make progress. Meeting once per week or once every other week, as is the norm for most special education services in the school, is simply not frequent enough to encourage change.

Some schools have dealt with this issue by naming two keyworkers. For instance, the social worker may meet with the child twice per week and the SLP may meet with him twice per week. It is great to have multiple communication partners within the school, and generally this works well if both keyworkers regularly communicate with one another. It should be expected that the child may progress slightly more slowly at first, as they must become desensitized to two different people instead of one.

The mental health professional outside of the school is responsible for:

1. Developing and maintaining the treatment plan through consultation with the school.
2. Training parents on strategies to increase communication with extended family/friends and in public settings.
3. Carrying out "brave practices" in public settings, such as ordering at restaurants, calling people on the phone, asking where to find items in the store, and approaching peers on the playground.

When seeking out a psychologist, behavior analyst or mental health professional to assist in the treatment, it is important to search for some key characteristics:

- Experience working with children, particularly children with anxiety disorders.
- Training and experience in behavioral therapy or cognitive behavioral therapy, and use of these as the main treatment modality.
- A willingness to learn about selective mutism (as it is treated slightly differently from other childhood anxiety disorders).
- A good rapport with the parent, child, and school, and a willingness to work productively with all three.

If you have a mental health professional with expertise or extensive experience in treating selective mutism in your area . . . you are *lucky*. These individuals can be found on the Selective Mutism Group website at www.selectivemutism.org (search under "Find Help"). Most areas do not have experts in their backyard, and therefore parents must find someone with the qualifications above through good, old-fashioned detective work (otherwise known as calling the psychologist's office and asking the right questions). If it is at all financially possible, parents are encouraged to make the decision regarding a treating professional on expertise, ability, and fit—not whether they accept the child's health insurance. While it is understandable that financial considerations are important and necessary for families, effective early intervention is so imperative that wasting time in an ineffective treatment might not be worth the money saved.

Parental responsibilities include:

1. Advocating for the child in the school setting.
2. Maintaining documentation of ***everything*** (school meetings, recommendations by the psychologist, teacher notes, progress notes, etc.).
3. Communicating with the teacher, keyworker, and clinical psychologist about progress.
4. Practicing regularly in public and with extended family and friends; this often means creating opportunities for the child to speak (this will be discussed later in Chapter Five).

BUILD RAPPORT

Once a treatment team is in place and the keyworker(s) have been determined, adults on the treatment team are encouraged to focus on building a positive rapport with the child. In general treatment outcome studies, the best predictor of treatment effectiveness is the relationship between patient and therapist. Selective mutism is no exception. This section on building rapport is mainly targeted to the treating professional or school personnel (e.g., teacher, keyworker, etc.), and the strategies outlined below are highly recommended for the first few sessions between the adult and a child with selective mutism. However, parents can also support the child's social and emotional growth by spending concentrated one-on-one time with the child with positive feedback for engaging in verbal interactions. Concentrated one-on-one time, or "special time" as I call it, is based on skills taught in parent child interaction therapy (PCIT), a therapeutic intervention developed to enhance the adult-child relationship by changing the interaction between the two parties. Although it is commonly used for young children with conduct disorder issues, it can also be very beneficial with children with selective mutism to provide positive and rewarding interactions with parents, allow for structured warm-up time with new individuals, and build rapport with novel adults (McNeil, 2010).

The "Do's" for rapport building or "special time" include:

- Play in a one-on-one setting. It is almost impossible to completely focus on a child and make them feel comfortable if there are other children, siblings, and adults entering and exiting the interaction.
- Play at the child's level and follow their lead. Activities that lend themselves well to this time include open-ended, creative play such as arts and crafts, constructional toys such as Legos, building blocks, and magnetic blocks, dollhouses with miniature people, and marble run sets. With older children, developmentally-appropriate (i.e., more complex) arts and crafts projects, board games, apps, etc. can be used to interact.
- Turn off all cell phones and distractions.
- PRIDE skills—rapport-building techniques that enhance the relationship.

PRIDE Skills

Skill		Examples
PRAISE **appropriate behavior**	Increases positive behavior Let us child know what you like Increases self-esteem Adds to warmth of the relationship Makes both adult and child feel good.	Terrific counting. You have wonderful ideas for this game. Thanks for showing me your picture. Thanks for letting me know. I love how you used your brave voice.
REFLECT **appropriate talk**	Shows the child you are really listening Demonstrates acceptance and understanding Improves child's speech Increases verbal communication	Child: I made a star Adult: Yes, you made a star. Child: (points at a dog picture) Adult: "You want me to see the dog picture. Thanks for showing me."
IMITATE **appropriate play**	Allows child to lead interaction Approves child's choice of play Shows child how to play with others (forms basis of taking turns/sharing)	Child: I am putting baby to bed. Parent: I will put sister to bed too. Child: (draws a sun in the sky) Parent: I am going to put a sun in my picture too.
DESCRIBE **appropriate behavior**	Allows child to lead Shows child you are interested Teaches concepts and vocabulary Models speech Holds child's attention	You are making a tower. You drew a smiling face. The cowboy looks happy. You are putting that together so well.
ENTHUSIAM	Demonstrates interest in child Models appropriate positive emotions Supports positive statements Strengthens positive relationship	Wow. That is great. That is super. (smiling)

"Don'ts for PRIDE skills

Rule	Reason	Examples
Don't give **COMMANDS**	Does not allow child to lead Results in a hierarchical relationship	Hand me that paper. Could you tell me the alphabet? The sun should really be yellow, not blue.
Don't ask **QUESTIONS**	Can cause the child's anxiety to increase. Many are commands or require an answer May reinforce avoidance	That is a blue one, right? What color is this? Are you drawing a castle? Do you want to play with the blocks?
Don't **CRITICIZE** (or correct)	Does not build rapport May lower the child's self-esteem Creates an unpleasant interaction	You are being naughty. Don't scribble on your paper That does not go that way

*Adapted from McNeil, 2010.

Many individuals are confused by the difference between reflections and behavioral descriptions. Reflections are a restatement of anything the child communicates, either verbally or nonverbally. For example, if the child made a verbal comment, a reflection would simply restate that comment (taking care not to turn the reflection into a question by adding an inflection to your voice). If the child nodded or pointed, a reflection would acknowledge that nonverbal communication. A behavioral description is much like the job of a sports announcer—it is providing the commentary of what is occurring in the play interaction.

"Special time" can be used to build rapport with a novel (or less familiar) adult. My first session(s) almost always include PRIDE skills, as the children are usually nervous and apprehensive when first meeting me, and my first goal in treatment is to build rapport. If there is one thing we know about children, it is that if they like you and respect you (and feel respected by you), they will try so very hard to accomplish the goals you set. If they don't like you or don't feel a rapport with you, they will likely do . . . nothing. PRIDE skills can be used by teachers when they first meet a new student, keyworkers when they begin working with the student in the school setting, clinical psychologists at the first session or few sessions to build rapport, parents to enhance the relationship and calm their child when the situation is overwhelming. The list of possible opportunities for use goes on and on.

The goal of "special time" with keyworkers or novel adults is to build rapport, but parents can also utilize "special time" to develop and practice interpersonal and social skills. This "special time" *with parents* can be particularly beneficial if paired with role-playing of typical, real-life communicative situations. Since speaking can be a high-stress and multi-faceted skill, scripting (e.g., developing an over-practiced language routine) can reduce anxiety and increase the likelihood that speech will just "slip out." For example, most children regularly go out to a restaurant to order, the café to buy a donut, or the store to purchase an item. For young children, role-playing of these activities can be done within pretend play situations. Some examples of role-playing could include:

- **Parent plays the role of storekeeper and the child "purchases" items in the store.** A script could include the child bringing the items to the counter and asking, "How much do I owe you?" After the parent responds with a price, the child hands over the money, which is good practice of handover-takeover (e.g., handing items to someone or taking items handed to them by others), says "Thank you," and takes the bag.

- **Parent plays the role of the barista at a café.** The child approaches the counter and the parent asks, "Hi, what can I get for you?" The child replies, "A donut and small apple juice" and hands over money. After handing back the change, the parent says, "Thank you." and the child replies back, "Thanks."

- **Parent plays the role of teacher in the classroom, and asks the child an academic question.** The child raises their hand and waits to be called on. When the "teacher" calls on them, the child responds verbally, and the parent praises the brave talking.

Of course, it is also great to switch roles so that the child has the opportunity to play the role of storekeeper, barista, and teacher. The key to this pretend play is over-practice; the child already has a concept of what to say in these situations (this is not new to them), but in order for the speech to come easily it must be over-practiced so that it is simply a natural response to the interaction. Additionally, repeated language routines in real life frequently help the child build confidence and become verbal. For example, a family I worked with went to the same Barnes and Noble® each week to order a cookie. It became part of their routine, and, with practice, their daughter was eventually able to order a cookie independently.

EDUCATING THE CHILD ABOUT ANXIETY

After a positive rapport has been developed with the child (this can be in the first session or may take several sessions) the next step is educating the child about selective mutism (although it is not necessary to use the specific term) and providing them with ways to communicate about anxiety. The description and psycho-education on anxiety may look very diverse depending on the age and understanding of the child. For individuals of all ages it is helpful to explain anxiety, discuss worries about speaking, and provide a scale for communication about "how hard" certain activities may be.

The steps in psycho-education include:

1. Explain anxiety.
2. Discuss how treatment will proceed.
3. Provide an anxiety rating scale.

For younger children:

I don't know if your mom or dad told you, but I work with a lot of kids who have a hard time getting their words out or talking to new people. Some kids say talking is hard because they are worried about how people might react when they talk, or maybe from feeling worried that they might not say the words right or people might not understand. Worries like that can make our stomach or head hurt, or it may make the words get stuck in our throat even when we want to talk. When that happens, it is good to start working with someone like me, because I teach kids how to feel braver and stronger. We do activities to build brave muscles.

I don't know if you have ever seen someone with REALLY big muscles, like this (show picture of weightlifter) *but these people are not just born with big muscles. Instead, they started off with almost no muscles at all. They wanted to get stronger, and so they lifted weights almost every day. They could not start out with huge weights, because they were not strong enough yet, but they lifted small weights every day until they built little muscles and got a little stronger. Then, they were able to lift medium-sized weights. At first, moving up to medium-sized weights was hard . . . and they had to push, and push, and push to get the weight up. But as they practiced every day, it got easier to lift the medium-sized weights, because their muscles were growing. Then, they were able to lift big weights.*

We are going to build our brave muscles in here in the same way. First, we start with brave practices that are easy, like nodding or shaking your head to answer my question. I can promise I will never make you do anything you cannot do—in fact, you get to be in charge of our brave muscle building. We will only move up to the next "weight" when you feel like you are strong enough. Your job is to work your hardest to get stronger and braver, and from what your mom and dad tell me, you are a really hard worker. The good news is that when you practice your brave work, we will have some cool prizes. Soon, the things that seemed a little hard will get easier and easier, because you will be getting stronger and stronger.

For older children/adolescents:

I met with your mom and dad recently, and they were telling me that they notice it is hard for you to talk to people sometimes in school and in public. I don't know if you realize this, but there are a lot of kids who have difficulty talking to people in public—in fact, when you ask kids and adults what their biggest fear is, the vast majority say speaking in public. Some kids and teenagers say that it is hard to talk because they are concerned about how others might react when they talk, or they are afraid to say something wrong or have people look at them funny. There is a name for this anxiety about talking to people in school or public; it is called selective mutism.

Sometimes anxiety is a good thing. If we did not have anxiety, people might not be careful when they drive, or not study for big tests, or might not be prepared for work. A little anxiety helps keep us safe and motivated. However, sometimes our brains give us too big of a "warning signal" when we are anxious. I am not sure if you have ever been in a school when a fire alarm was pulled as a prank, but I have. Our class filed out the door and into the parking lot, because the siren was alerting us to go and we did not know that there wasn't really a fire. Sometimes our brains send us the alarm signal when it is not really necessary. We call these "brain tricks." The good news is, we can start controlling these brain tricks and get stronger and braver through slow practice of things that are hard.

Let me give you an example. If I were learning how to ride a bike, I would not just jump on a regular bike and ride down a huge hill. That would be way too scary. Instead, I would start with riding on a flat sidewalk with training wheels, and when that was easy I might take the training wheels off and have someone hold the back of the bike steady while I ride. When that is easy, I could ask them to let go but still ride on a flat sidewalk until I was good. Then, I would feel comfortable to ride on increasingly bigger hills, because I have practiced. The thing that seemed too hard at first (riding a regular bike down a big hill) now seems easy because I practiced the little steps slowly.

That is what I am hoping you and I can do together. My job is to help you with the slow steps—to be your coach. I will never ask you to do anything you cannot do—in fact, you get to be in charge of letting me know when you are ready to move to the next step. Your job is to try as hard as you can to be brave even when it is hard, because if you just stick in there and practice, it quickly gets easier and easier, until it is not hard at all anymore.

It is important to remember that education on anxiety is not something you do one single time. These statements will need to be repeated and revisited with children several times. The more kids understand *why* they are practicing and *what* the eventual goal is (for them to feel braver and stronger), the more internally motivated they are. At times, it is helpful to use a visual representation similar to the conceptualization of selective mutism. I use an "avoidance cycle" and "brave cycle" to teach older children about the reasoning behind brave practices.

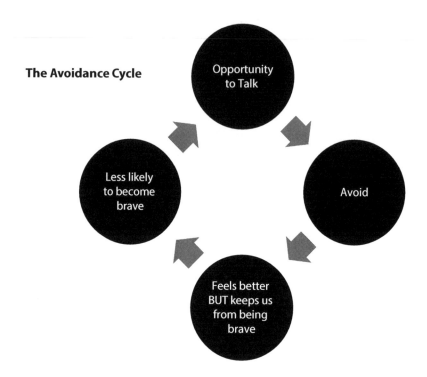

Next, kids are taught to assess and report their own anxiety level. A five-point scale provides enough information without being overwhelming to children. For younger children and visual learners, I use a visual 1-5 scale. This may take the form of a mercury thermometer or a progression of five faces (progressing from happy to sad). *The Incredible 5-Point Scale* is a wonderful resource for assisting kids in visually understanding how to rate their anxiety (Dunn Buron, 2007). I generally do not ask children to rate how "scary" or "anxiety-provoking" an activity is, as many children with selective mutism do not describe feelings of "fear" or "anxiety." Instead, children are asked how "hard" they think it will be or how "hard" it really was. Ratings occur at four different time points in treatment:

- At the start of treatment, to help build a step-wise ladder (communication ladder) of communication activities. It is helpful to know what the child perceives as especially hard, since my estimation of the difficulty level of the activity and their perception may not be the same.

- Prior to "brave practices"—"Okay, we get to practice answering a short question from Ms. Mensel. How hard do you think this will be?"

- After a "brave practice" has been completed—"That was great. Now tell me how hard it really was to answer that question from Ms. Mensel."

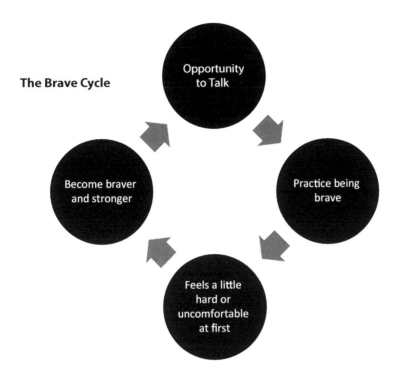

• As a summary of progression in treatment, such as a reminder of how far the child has come—"Do you remember that answering me used to be a 4, but now you have told me that it is down to a 1. You have gotten so much braver and stronger. You are really building those brave muscles."

Asking a child to report how hard they believe an activity will be and how hard it really was provides an opportunity for feedback on the "brain tricks" mentioned earlier. A key characteristic of anxiety disorders is an over-estimation of how bad the feared activity will be. Ninety percent of the time, children will respond that the actual practice was much easier than they had expected it to be, and it allows the adult to respond, "Wow—that practice ended up being easier than you thought it would be. We should remember this—our brains sometimes trick us in to believing that our brave practices will be harder than they really end up being. Next time you think a practice will be hard, can I remind you of this experience and how you are a lot braver than you think?"

Of course, all kids have the occasional experience of a practice that is just as hard as, or even harder, than they had hypothesized. When that occurs, adults can again provide helpful, constructive feedback including:

"Okay, it is good for us to know that answering Ms. Mensel was as hard as you thought it was going to be. I am so impressed that even though you thought it was going to be a 3, and you were right in your rating, you were still able to do it. That just shows what a brave kid you are, that you will try something even though it is kind of hard. That is the kind of practice that makes us so much braver and stronger."

Or:

"So you had thought it would be a 3, but when you really went up to answer Ms. Mensel, it jumped up to a 5. Yikes. Let's think of a way that you could still practice being brave, but maybe something a little easier than answering with two words. Maybe we could have you answer with one short word or just a sound, or maybe we could have Ms. Mensel turn away from you as you answer. What do you think?"

CONTINGENCY MANAGEMENT

I know, I know—you have already tried reward systems, and they have not worked. Many parents report to me that they have tried reward systems in the past. They offered their child a new iPod® and a pony if the child would just talk . . . but that still did not work to increase speech. If you are reading this book, you have probably already realized that for most children with selective mutism, reward systems by themselves are useless. However, contingency management can be a very useful tool in conjunction with a good intervention plan.

Contingency management: Making verbalizations more rewarding and nonverbal responding or a lack of responding less rewarding.

We have all done it. We have all made it very easy for the child to get what they want and need, and to convey information via facial expressions, writing, nonverbal gestures, or another mode of silent communication. This allowance does help the child become comfortable and successful in the school setting. It does not, nonetheless, increase verbalizations. I recently had a session with a third grader with selective mutism. We were discussing his progression to talking to peers in school and a few specific adults, but he has yet to speak to his teacher. When I asked him what was keeping him from including his teacher in his "talking circle," he replied, "She gives me the white board and lets me write all of my answers." This teacher was making nonverbal responding very rewarding for him.

There are many ways of utilizing contingency management when working with kids with selective mutism. First, we need to offer them the opportunity to talk, usually through asking questions that prompt or encourage a verbal response. The best way to do this is through forced-choice (or multiple-choice) questions. When children with selective mutism are asked a question in a yes/no format, it immediately and naturalistically offers up a nonverbal response (nodding or shaking their head). When they are ask a question in an open-ended manner, it may be overwhelming—the child may be caught trying to decide how to respond, what the "correct" response is, what the asker really wants to hear, etc. Instead, if the child is provided with a few options for a response, we increase the likelihood that he or she will answer verbally. Trying to change our questions to forced-choice takes some practice. Let us try changing a few yes/no and open-ended questions to forced-choice questions.

Open-Ended Example:	"What did you do this weekend?"
Forced Choice Question:	<u>"Did you ride your bike, play videogames, or something different this weekend?"</u>
Yes/No Example:	"Do you like dogs?"
Forced Choice Question:	<u>"Do you like dogs or not like dogs?"</u>

| Open-Ended Question: | "What is your favorite color?" |
| Forced Choice Question: | |

| Open-Ended Question: | "How is your little brother feeling?" |
| Forced Choice Question: | |

| Yes/No Question: | "Did you dress up this year for Halloween? |
| Forced Choice Question: | |

| Yes/No Question: | "Do you want to work on your math right now? |
| Forced Choice Question: | |

Beware—sometimes we may not provide the "right" response, and the child may not answer. If the child does not respond, you may first want to change your possible answers. For example, if you ask a child, "What do you like best—dogs or cats?" and the child does not like either dogs or cats, they may not answer you. You may need to revise the question to, "What do you like better—dogs, cats, both, or neither?"

When a child responds to a forced-choice question, that response should first be reflected. Reflection consists simply of rewording or repeating the child's response back to him. Then, the adult verbally reinforces the response. It is always important to reinforce the child verbally and through your body language. Many children with SM do not like to receive a lot of overt praise for their brave behaviors. They fear people making a big deal out of their talking, which is one of the reasons they avoid speech. In a recent workshop, a participant described a situation in which a child with SM in her school had finally spoken to the teacher. In her excitement, the teacher stopped class immediately, brought everyone's attention to the child and congratulated him with a huge amount of praise for talking, cancelled the rest of the class day, and threw a party. The child did not return to school for two weeks . . . and when he did return he never spoke again. *Please don't be that teacher.*

Verbal reinforcement should be relatively low-key and matter-of-fact, such as saying, "Thanks for letting me know" or "Great job using your brave voice." In order not to call attention to the child, I may just give a thumbs-up or a pat on the back, or just whisper in their ear what a great job they did.

A sample interaction consisting of forced-choice questions, reflections, and labeled praise for responding could include:

Mom: *What would you like to do today—go to the park, play on the trampoline, or something different?*

Child: *Go to the park.*

Mom: *Go to the park! Thanks for letting me know. I love going to the park. Should we go to Whittier Park or the park downtown?*

Child: *I want to go to the one with the big slides.*

Mom: *Oh, the one with the big slides—that is a really fun one. That's Whittier Park. Are you going to try going down the biggest slide, or the medium-sized slides?*

Child: *I'm going to go down the biggest one this time.*

Mom: *Thanks for telling me that you want to go on the biggest one. You are getting so brave.*

After we have increased the likelihood that the child will respond to us verbally, we must have a reinforcement system in place. The most common reinforcers or rewards are:

- **Obtaining desired outcome**—the child gets what they want through verbal communication as opposed to using nonverbal communication to get all needs met.

- **Verbal Reinforcement**—verbal praise or body language suggesting pleasure/proudness.

- **Tangible Reinforcement**—prizes such as toys, special outings, or belongings.

- **Reinforcement through privileges**—privileges the child would not normally receive, such as staying up later, watching extra TV or playing extra videogames, picking out a game to play with their mother, maintenance of their cell phone/car/computer, etc.

Reinforcement in the form of privileges or tangible items best comes through a structured reward system. This could take the form of earning "brave bucks," stickers, poker chips, etc. for brave behaviors. It is important to define what the child is specifically working on—do they earn stickers for making sounds? Whispering? Blowing air? Do these culminate in a reward after earning a certain number? Is this "reward" really rewarding to the child?

While parents and interventionists may want to start off rewarding more frequently occurring behaviors, such as nonverbal communication, in order to get the child invested and responsive to the reward system, it is important that the reward system switches quickly to reinforcements only for verbal behaviors.

Here are some examples of contingency management with a child:

> **Shawn is a 5-year-old boy with selective mutism who loves Legos®.** *When starting the intervention, his mother was instructed to stop purchasing Lego sets for any reason other than rewards for brave behaviors (i.e., no Legos as Christmas gifts, gifts from family members, etc.). Since Shawn was already consistently nonverbally responding to the psychologist during the first session, the psychologist explained that the brave work today would be blowing air (since this is a pre-requisite to speech). The psychologist and Shawn did several activities to practice, including cotton ball races, straw painting, and blowing up balloons. For each blow, Shawn earned a Lego-themed sticker, with the understanding that if he earned ten stickers in the session (a number the psychologist felt he could likely accomplish), he would earn a desired Lego set. With each blow, the psychologist also made comments such as, "Wow, you are great at brave work." "You are such a great air blower." and "I love how loudly you are blowing." as well as thumbs up and lots of smiles and engagement. At the end of the session, when Shawn reached ten stickers, he was immediately given his new Lego set.*

Gina is a 6-year-old girl who enjoys dressing up as a princess. *She very occasionally whispers a response in the school setting if the interaction is one-on-one, and the school and parents wish to increase this speech. The social worker makes a cardboard "necklace" with several small pieces of Velcro®, and the teacher is given many beautiful "jewels" with Velcro on the back. Each time Gina whispers to anyone at school, she immediately receives a jewel to add to her necklace, and her goal is to fill up the necklace by the end of the day to obtain a prize from her mother when she returns home.*

Stephanie is a 14-year-old girl whose behavior is reinforced by time on her iPad®. *Her time on the iPad is earned by the number of questions and answers she gives in class that day. Her parents and teachers have set up a system by which they all have access to a private Google® document. Each time Stephanie raises her hand to answer a question in class, or approaches her teachers with a question, comment, or need, the teachers open the Google document and record. When Stephanie arrives home, her parents check the Google document and she is given ten minutes of play time for each verbalization to teachers.*

There are many possible pit-falls of reward systems. The most common ones include:

- Rewarding with identified reinforcers without the occurrence of the goal behavior (e.g., if Shawn's grandparents had purchased three Lego sets for him on his birthday, Legos may no longer be rewarding).

- Trying to use rewards that are not reinforcing for the child—if a child does not really care if they use the iPad, it is unlikely that they will work for that particular reward.

- Not changing the reward system periodically—everything gets old eventually, even access to iPads. Reward systems must be consistently changed and updated (i.e., changes in reinforcers as well as criteria/behaviors to be reinforced as the child progresses).

- Inconsistency in doling out the reward—rewards should be as immediate as possible. I realize that life is busy, and you don't always have time to run to the store or take the child out for a special dinner. Imagine, however, that you worked all week for a paycheck, and then your boss "did not have time" or "forgot" to pay you. Most adults would not continue to put forth effort to work at that establishment.

- Making the goal behavior too difficult to accomplish—the goal behavior for reward systems MUST be attainable. If it is not, it will only frustrate you and the child.

- Giving the feared back-handed compliment, "I like how you used your voice with grandma on the phone today. Why could you not do that before?"

Some ideas for rewards (circle any that might be rewarding to your child or the child you are working with):

- Candy
- Money
- Staying up 15 minutes later
- Slurpee® from 7 Eleven®
- Chuckie Cheese® (plus $10 for tokens)
- Pick restaurant
- Eat dessert for dinner
- Extra "special time" with parents
- Go to library
- Go to toy store (with $15 to spend)
- Go bowling
- Ice cream
- Extra TV time
- Extra video game time
- Extra computer time
- Trip to McDonalds® (or favorite restaurant)

- Pick what is cooked for dinner
- Buy new video game
- Rent DVD
- Rent video game
- Go to the movies
- Pick out of surprise prize box
- Package of gum
- Make popcorn
- Go to water park
- Go to a bounce house
- Family game night
- _____
- _____
- _____
- _____

TOOLS OF THE TRADE

Research continually demonstrates that the most effective intervention for selective mutism is behavioral treatment using desensitization (Oerbeck, 2013; Vecchio, 2009). Behavioral interventions are effective in reducing anxiety and increasing verbal communication. In a study on the effectiveness of interventions for selective mutism, the researchers compared behavioral intervention to other treatment types, including medication, family systems therapy, and psychodynamic interventions (Pionek Stone, 2002). The study found that behaviorally oriented treatments show the largest improvements. The data also indicated that intervening soon after symptoms emerge leads to larger improvements than waiting to treat. Overall, age of symptom onset, speed of intervention after onset, and quality of treatment were the most important factors leading to increased speech.

In a recent study, Bergman and colleagues (2013) examined the effectiveness of behavior therapy for selective mutism. The children who participated had moderate to severe symptom levels. After treatment using this behavioral approach, parents and teachers reported that the children had increased their communication and were speaking more at school. Parents also noted that the children's anxiety had decreased. These results were corroborated by blind raters (raters who were unfamiliar with the children and whether they had received treatment or no treatment). The researchers followed up with the children three months after treatment and found that gains were maintained.

Behavioral intervention is based on desensitization, or slow, systematic steps toward facing a fear. Currently, the reason that the child with selective mutism is not speaking is because their fear is so great and the prompts and demands placed on them exceed their ability to manage their anxiety and respond. However, these prompts and demands can be decreased to a manageable level, which allows for success and increases motivation.

Desensitization for selective mutism is not so different from desensitization to any other fear. For example, if a child was afraid of dogs, a parent could practice slow steps with the child to increase her confidence and decrease anxiety about dogs. It is important that these steps start easy and get progressively more difficult or anxiety-provoking. Steps might include:

1. Thinking about dogs
2. Looking at pictures or videos of dogs
3. Watching real dogs who are far away
4. Getting progressively closer to a dog
5. Touching the dog
6. Petting, feeding, and taking the dog for a walk

With each step, we would expect increased anxiety, but as long as it was a manageable step, and as long as the practice was consistent, the individual would begin to relax and perform that step with confidence. We would then know that it was time to take the next step. In order for the step to be manageable, we may need to break it down into smaller steps, such as looking at cartoon/silly pictures of dogs, real pictures of dogs, cartoon videos of dogs, real videos of dogs, and then real videos of the dogs the child actually comes into contact with.

Desensitization of selective mutism works in a very similar manner. Instead of focusing on the end result (talking to many different people), we focus first on a small step that the child can perform, and move slowly toward more complex, difficult behaviors. There are two main "tools" in the desensitization toolbox of the clinician: stimulus fading and shaping.

Stimulus fading is a process by which the clinician takes pre-existing speech and transfers that speech to new places and new people. The goal of stimulus fading is to change *where*, *when*, and *with whom* the child communicates. *Shaping* involves reinforcing successive approximations of speech, starting with the way in which the child is currently able to communicate. The goal of shaping is slowly increasing *what* the child is able to communicate. We can determine the most effective intervention(s) based on the diagnostic interview and evaluation completed in the assessment phase.

	Speech Frequency (How frequently?)	Communication Partners (Who?)	Setting Variable (Where?)	Intervention Recommended
Type 1	Limited	Most people	Most environments	Contingency management
Type 2	Typical	One or limited people	Most environments	Stimulus fading of new people in specific environments
Type 3	Typical	Most people	One environment	Stimulus fading of environments
Type 4	Limited	One or limited people	One environment	Stimulus fading of new people into comfortable environment AND stimulus fading of environments
Type 5	No speech	No people	No environments	Shaping AND Stimulus fading of new people and environments

*Adapted from (Shriver, 2011).

Based on the child's presentation of speech outside of the home, we can generally fit children into one of these five categories. Think of your child or the child you are working with—what category do they generally fall into?

_____Type 1 Kids: These children speak to most people in most places, but are hesitant, quiet, or short in their responses. They may be whisperers, and may need a fair amount of time to warm up. While the child may be a consistent responder to direct questions, especially in one-on-one situations, they don't usually initiate (such as raising their hands in class or asking the teacher about their weekend). For these children, contingency management (or making speaking more reinforcing and silence less reinforcing) is recommended as a main intervention approach.

_____ Type 2 Kids: These children have fairly typical speech—they speak in a normal tone of voice, with long responses and even occasional or frequent initiations. They speak in this normal way in most environments, IF they are speaking to one or a few specific people. For example, they may speak to their mother in almost all environments (i.e., school, restaurants, stores, family friend's homes) in a normal voice, but don't direct that speech to others. For these children, stimulus fading is used to transition existing speech from the current communication partner to other new communication partners, especially in environments where the speech already occurs easily.

_____ Type 3 Kids: These children have typical speech with most people, but only in one (or limited) environments. A child with this presentation may talk to anyone who comes into their home, but that speech does not generalize to outside of the home. Alternatively, after they are comfortable in the Social Worker's office at school they may talk to anyone who enters into that room, but as soon as the child leaves the room, all communication ceases. For these children, stimulus fading is used to transition that existing speech to new places.

_____ Type 4 Kids: These children have limited speech with only one or a few people in only one or a few places. For example, these children may talk to the speech pathologist in her office, but when anyone else enters the room OR when they leave the room, the child becomes silent again. For these children, stimulus fading is used to transition speech from current communication partners to new people as well as to move pre-existing speech to other environments.

_____ Type 5 Kids: These children generally do not speak to anyone in any environments outside of the home setting. For these children, the intervention must start with shaping in order to obtain speech, and then stimulus fading can also be used to transition this speech to new environments and with new people.

STIMULUS FADING

Stimulus fading is, in my experience, the easiest and most "naturalistic" way of increasing speech for children with selective mutism, if it is a possibility given the characteristics of the child (see chart above). The general idea of fading is to obtain speech from the child using an individual with whom the child currently speaks (this may be the parent, keyworker, or other relative) and "fading" that speech into a new situation (e.g., a new environment or including a new communication partner). First, we must determine to whom the child speaks and where the child speaks.

Who does the child talk to already? This could include parents, relatives, school personnel, peers, etc.

Already talks to:

_____ in _____
Person (e.g., mom, dad, teacher)   Environments (e.g., classroom, private office in school, school sidewalk, playground)

_____ in _____
Person (e.g., mom, dad, teacher)   Environments (e.g., classroom, private office in school, school sidewalk, playground)

_____ in _____
Person (e.g., mom, dad, teacher)   Environments (e.g., classroom, private office in school, school sidewalk, playground)

_____ in _____
Person (e.g., mom, dad, teacher)   Environments (e.g., classroom, private office in school, school sidewalk, playground)

_____ in _____
Person (e.g., mom, dad, teacher)   Environments (e.g., classroom, private office in school, school sidewalk, playground)

_____ in _____
Person (e.g., mom, dad, teacher)   Environments (e.g., classroom, private office in school, school sidewalk, playground)

What environments or with whom would it be helpful for speech to occur (where it does not currently occur)?

_____ in _____

Person (e.g., mom, dad, teacher)   Environments (e.g., classroom, private office in school, school sidewalk, playground)

_____ in _____

Person (e.g., mom, dad, teacher)   Environments (e.g., classroom, private office in school, school sidewalk, playground)

_____ in _____

Person (e.g., mom, dad, teacher)   Environments (e.g., classroom, private office in school, school sidewalk, playground)

_____ in _____

Person (e.g., mom, dad, teacher)   Environments (e.g., classroom, private office in school, school sidewalk, playground)

_____ in _____

Person (e.g., mom, dad, teacher)   Environments (e.g., classroom, private office in school, school sidewalk, playground)

Stimulus fading allows us to take the speech that already exists, such as speaking to a parent in a closed-office setting of the school, and add in a new communication partner or move to a new environment. Examples of both adding in new communication partners and moving to new environments are included. Please note that all steps do not have to be accomplished in one day. Instead, movement to the next step should only occur when the current step seems comfortable and easy for the child. That may mean that each step takes three minutes or three hours, we must not move more quickly than the child can tolerate. Do not move to the next step of the stimulus fading procedure if the child stops talking. Instead, stop where you are and the communication partner should re-establish speech. For instance, if the child is fading into a new environment and becomes mute, extremely quiet, or generally nonresponsive, the communication partner should stop and try to re-elicit speech before moving forward. If a new person is fading into an interaction and the child becomes mute, the person fading in should stop their progression into the room (just stay where they are) and the communication partner should try to get the child engaged and talking again. Only when the child looks relatively comfortable and is speaking again should the fading restart.

The fading procedure is generally used in a naturalistic sense, meaning that the intent is not explained in detail to the child. For example, a parent might let the child know that they will be playing in Ms. Smith's room today, and that Ms. Smith may have some work to do in the room while they are playing. If the goal of stimulus fading is to transfer speech to a new environment, the communication partner may just try to keep up the interaction, conversation, or play while slowly moving to a new area.

Example Stimulus Fading—New Communication Partners

The goal is to fade a new communication partner (NCP) into the room while the child continues to use appropriate speech directed toward the mother but within NCP's earshot. The mother's job is to keep the child talking through fun activities that encourage speech and forced-choice questions (while the NCP slowly enters the room).

- Mother and child should have some time to "warm up" in the room, playing and talking alone with the door closed or almost closed.

- NCP begins fading into the room when the mother has obtained an appropriate volume of consistent speech from the child. The NCP begins by simply opening the door and walking around and in front of the door, so as to make her presence known. The NCP should NOT respond in any way to what the child says or act as if they are attending to the child (no eye contact, no attention, no responses to the child's activity or speech).

- The NCP should very slowly enter the room, as far away from the child as possible, and busy themselves (i.e., type on the computer, pick up the room, or do paperwork). If the child begins to discontinue speaking or shows other general signs of anxiety, slow the entrance or stay in the same position for several minutes until the anxiety is reduced and speech resumes.

- The NCP should slowly start making their way toward the child/mother by finding things to do in closer proximity to their interaction, but should continue to pay no attention to the child.

- When the NCP is close to the interaction and the child has maintained speech, he/she can begin silently to attend to the interaction (just watching without commenting).

- If the child tolerates attention to their speech, the NCP can begin to comment, reflect, or respond to what the child is saying. For example, if the child tells the parent that they picked a blue card, the NCP could reflect, "Oh, you picked a blue card." If the child tells the mother that he played his new videogame last night, the NCP could comment, "You played your new game—that sounds like fun."

- When this seems comfortable and minimally anxiety-provoking, the NCP can begin peppering in occasional forced-choice questions.

- When the child is consistently responding to the NCP, the parent can begin fading out of the room, leaving the NCP and the child. This should not be attempted until the child appears to be fairly comfortable in speaking with the NCP. If necessary, use the same gradual fading in process described above—only in reverse.

If the NCP is unable to complete all steps in one session, they could start outside the room at the next session but attempt to fade in more quickly. As the child's anxiety will likely spontaneously return somewhat at the beginning of each session (although less and less will be present each time), the NCP should take care to be responsive to the anxiety.

Example Stimulus Fading—New Environments

The goal is to transition speech from the current location to a new location, using someone with whom the child already speaks comfortably.

1. Begin in an environment that is associated with speech, such as the parent's car.
2. Play a verbal game or engage the child in an interesting conversation to elicit speech (e.g., 20 questions, I Spy, taking turns telling jokes).
3. Instead of quickly exiting the car, move more slowly, first just opening the car door and attempting to maintain speech.
4. Slowly exit the car, keeping the child engaged, and stay near the car.
5. Take very slow steps toward the door, keeping the child engaged in the verbalizations.
6. Maintain speech as long as possible, and praise the child for using their voice in a new environment.
7. With each new stimulus fading attempt, the goal should be to move the speech further.

Fading can be used in a number of different ways. For example, fading can be used in conjunction with video or audiotaping. If a child is willing to be videotaped, the fading procedure on page 118 should be used to fade the child toward speech with a new communication partner. A similar technique could be used with the phone, FaceTime®, Skype®, and other technology.

Example Fading via Voice Recordings

1. Teacher (or New Communication Partner—NCP) tapes herself asking a question via voice recording (the sillier the better). Voice recordings could be made on cell phones, voice recording devices, taped on an answering machine, etc.
2. Child answers privately (at home or in a different room) on a voice recorder and asks a question (can be the same question or a different question); send to teacher and teacher responds. Continue asking and answering each other remotely via voice recording.
3. Teacher asks a question and child responds in the room (and back and forth).
4. Teacher slowly moves closer as child responds via voice recording.
5. Teacher asks a question and child responds right next to her.
6. (Fade voice recorder)—teacher asks a question while phone is sitting on desk away from face and child responds.
7. Both pretend to hit the record button but teacher asks a question and child responds.

SHAPING

For those children who are not yet speaking to anyone in any environment outside of the home, whose speech is very inconsistent or extremely quiet, or who have been involved in unsuccessful stimulus fading procedures, shaping speech is the best option. Shaping (otherwise known as the building of a communication ladder) involves breaking speech down into small, manageable steps, and reinforcing the slow, steady steps toward speech. Just as we would not expect a child with an intense fear of dogs to be able to immediately approach and play with a new dog, we cannot expect a child with selective mutism to approach their teacher and ask for help. Instead, we must make the practices manageable.

A communication ladder (shaping procedure) can involve many small steps. Intervention should start where the child currently is functioning and progress up the ladder slowly but consistently. The very basis of the communication ladder may be simply following directions, especially for the child who freezes entirely in interactions and cannot even consistently respond nonverbally. The highest rung on the communication ladder is spontaneous initiation of communication and starting/maintaining conversations.

The communication ladder is based on three principals:

Principal One: Speaking in gradual steps helps the fear go away.

a. This is called exposure, but it's really just structured practice. It's sort of like learning to ride a bike—at first, you start easy, with training wheels; then, parents hold on to the bike while you ride slowly with two wheels; eventually, you are riding alone slowly and then more quickly. At each step you gain confidence and that thing that was scary isn't so scary anymore.

b. The first step is identifying what is feared (where it is scary to speak, who it is scary to speak to, etc.).

c. Then a ladder is created starting with least difficult scenarios (e.g., mimicking speech or nonverbal communication), going up eventually to really difficult scenarios (e.g., initiating speech with a stranger).

d. The ladder begins in the clinic or office, and when the child is successful, that step of the ladder is generalized to other environments (e.g., in public and at school).

e. At each step, the child gains confidence and a "scary" situation is faced, thereby making it not so difficult anymore.

Principal Two: Success is rewarded.

a. We all like rewards when we work hard, so communication ladders also have rewards.

b. When successful on the current step of the ladder, children are either immediately given a small reward (e.g., very small toy/candy) or are given a token (e.g., sticker, poker chip) that they can cash in later for a slightly bigger reward.

c. Furthermore, parents, keyworkers, and others in the child's life give them verbal reinforcement for their "bravery."

d. Finally, it is intrinsically rewarding to be successful, and this increases motivation to continue making progress on the communication ladder.

Principal Three: Keeping up the momentum is important.

a. We can keep up the momentum by communicating about what the child has been successful on, and what "step" of the ladder he/she is currently working on (that way, we don't have stagnation in one environment—if the child is communicating with single words in the clinic, they should be working on that step in public and in school).

b. We can also keep up the momentum by being consistent and rewarding improvements in attempted speech.

On the following page is a list of possible steps on the communication ladder, along with many ideas of activities that could be utilized while practicing each step. These steps should be done playfully and in a fun, interactive manner, so integrating them into play or enjoyable interaction is essential.

Following directions

- Simon Says
- Arts and crafts
- Board games
- Cooking
- Dot-to-dot
- Barrier activities (activities in which two people are trying to achieve the same result without seeing each other—a physical barrier is between the two and the speaker gives instructions for the listener to create scenes, make things, or recreate a picture)
- Classroom helper
- Red light/green light game
- Scavenger hunt
- Sorting tasks
- Fun with Directions™ app

Gestures (writing, pointing, nodding/shaking head, shrugging shoulders, etc.)

- Charades
- Songs with hand movements (e.g., Itsy Bitsy Spider)
- Thumbs up/thumbs down
- *Where's Waldo®* books
- I Spy
- Picture Exchange Communication System (PECS)—teaching the child to give a picture of the desired item or activity to the communication partner
- Assistive Technology Devices (technology the child can use to communicate, such as Tap To Talk™ apps or typing programs)
- Yes/no questions
- Kids on Stage™ board game
- Pictureka™ board game
- Making choices ("Do you want this one or this one?")

Making noise (without the use of the mouth.)

- Clapping
- Stomping
- Snapping
- Musical instruments that don't require the mouth (e.g., drums, tambourine, cymbals, etc.)
- Rain sound
- Tapping foot to the music

Making faces

- Mirrored faces
- Making feelings faces or silly faces
- Oral-motor exercises
- Funny Faces™ board game

Blowing air

- Cotton ball races
- Bubbles
- Balloons
- Pinwheels
- Straw painting
- Blowing tissues
- Free Candle™ app
- Blow Balloon Pop™ app
- Blow Blow™ app

Voiceless sounds (s, t, p, k, h, f, sh, ch, voiceless th)

- Snake sound
- Cotton ball race with sounds
- Flat tire sound
- Pinwheel with sounds

Voiced sounds and/or environmental/animal noises

- All other sounds, but bilabials first (i.e., those sounds that do not require a large mouth opening, such as the *m*, *b*, and *w* sound)

Sound combinations leading to words

- Shape discrete sounds into sound combinations and into words
- Start with y/es and n/o sounds, since they are easily functional

- y/es and n/o sounds discretely
- discrete sounds closer in proximity
- sounds combined
- mimicked yes/no
- yes/no questions with a cued response (e.g., "Are you a girl? Say yes.")

One word responses (forced choice when possible as opposed to open-ended)

- Board games
- Making choices
- Fill in the blank or complete the sentence
- Sparklefish™ app
- Super Duper™ apps (www.superduperinc.com)
- Go Fish!™
- Hangman
- Old Maid
- Battleship™
- Smarty Ears™ apps (www.smartyearsapps.com)
- Hot/cold game
- What's missing games—show the child several pictures or objects, ask them not to look while you remove one, and they guess what is missing
- Uno™
- Counting tasks
- Fact or Crap™ card game

Multiple word responses and longer utterances

- Chinese whispers or Telephone game—one person quietly tells something to another, and the message is passed around until the last player says it aloud
- Reading, songs
- TV jingles
- "Tell me about . . ."
- Role playing
- What's wrong pictures
- Finish the story
- Barrier games
- Carrier phrases (phrases in which the first few words remain the same and the last one changes, such as "I see a ____," "I found a ____," I have a ____", and "I made a ____.")
- Sequencing cards
- Singing

Initiating

- Puppet Pals™ app
- Show and Tell™ game
- Headbanz™
- 20 Questions
- Child gives you instructions (for making crafts, playing videogames, etc.)
- Taking turns asking questions
- Knock-knock jokes
- Person bingo (see page 122)
- Guess Who?™ board game
- Wordless books—telling the story
- Child interviews you
- Retelling stories
- Toontastic™ app
- Requesting help
- Story starter cards or cubes
- Communicative temptations (setting up the environment to tempt the child to communicate, such as arranging an obstacle to a desired object, "accidentally" moving the child's piece in a board game, or not providing an important part of a craft)
- Acting out a story

Starting and maintaining conversations

- First scripted, then spontaneous
- Use social stories or social skills books, such as those by Jed Baker, Ph.D. (director of the Social Skills Training Project)
- Role play

Each child is different, and will need to start at a different level with different people in different environments. First, these steps should be practiced one-on-one with new communication partners, and then the existing speech can be faded into new places and new people can be faded into the interaction. Even within these steps, smaller steps could be added if the next step produces quite a bit of anxiety and avoidance. For example, many children have difficulty blowing air but can blow up a balloon. The blowing air step could be broken down to blowing up a balloon, then cutting the tip (the part that you blow into) off of the balloon and blowing. The tip could be cut off more and more until very little of the balloon is remaining and the child is essentially blowing air. Additionally, many steps can be easily integrated into one interaction. For instance, if the child is practicing blowing a pinwheel and is doing well, the interventionist may recommend "changing how we are blowing" to the "sssss" sound or the "puhpuhpuh" sound to make the pinwheel spin. Thus, we are moving from blowing air to voiceless sounds seamlessly.

It is time to take the next step on the ladder when two criteria are met:

- The child is consistently following through with the activity with very little hesitation or prompting.
- The child does not look anxious about completing their brave work.

If you are working on one-word responses, and the child is covering his mouth each time he answers, it is not time to move to the next step. If you are blowing air and the child is only blowing air when you are working with balloons, but is unable to blow into a pinwheel or tissue, he needs more practice on this step. There is no specific number of practices or amount of time that corresponds with moving on; you must observe anxiety level and compliance.

Each new session will likely require a warm-up period. This warm-up period should consist of a reminder of the brave work completed in the last session, as well as praise for the progress made thus far. Then, the child should begin brave practices several steps below where they ended in the last session and quickly progress forward. For example, if the child ended the last session on blowing air, the next session may begin with practicing making body sounds and facial expressions.

Let us develop a communication ladder for a specific child. Imagine this being done with a new communication partner, one-on-one, in a private setting. The first step should be one which the child currently completes consistently one-on-one. If a child already uses gestures with this person consistently, don't move back down on the ladder to following directions. If the child already makes environmental or animal sounds with the person, start there and move up the ladder. Add activity ideas that the child might particularly enjoy under each step on the communication ladder (use the ideas above to personalize it to your child, student, or patient).

Communication Ladder for _____

Step One: _____

- _____
- _____
- _____
- _____

Step Two: _____

- _____
- _____
- _____
- _____

Step Three: _____

- _____
- _____
- _____
- _____

Step Four: _____

- _____
- _____
- _____
- _____

Step Five: _____

- _____
- _____
- _____
- _____

Step Six: _____

- _____
- _____
- _____
- _____

Step Seven: _____

- _____
- _____
- _____
- _____

Step Eight: _____

- _____
- _____
- _____
- _____

When working with a child, the interventionist can use a sheet with a ladder on it, such as on page 120. First, write the current step, as well as the steps we have already completed, on the sheet. This allows the interventionist to visually demonstrate the child's progress in the "brave ladder." At each new session, start one to two steps back on the ladder from where the last session ended, in order to help the child "warm up" again. When working with an older child who may not like a ladder, the interventionist could draw a visual of stair steps, train tracks, or branches on a tree to illustrate movement in the direction of becoming braver and stronger.

The communication ladder generally works best at first when done without the parent in the room. When prompted to respond to a question or practice a step in the ladder, many children immediately turn to their parent to provide a response. They have become so accustomed to avoiding interactions with novel adults by looking to parents to respond and interact for them that they immediately attempt this avoidance tactic. Parents are so used to responding and communicating for the child that they may automatically answer or jump in and speak for the child. Thus, unless there is significant separation anxiety, I request that the parent return to the waiting room during the session. At the end of the session, I bring the parent back in to the room and practice the current step or goal with the parent in the room. Many times, children who were easily speaking with me without the parent in the room suddenly regress. This is NOT because of a family dynamic issue or a dislike of the parents; instead, it is likely a type of performance anxiety—the child has to become desensitized to the parent seeing them speak to me. This should be considered a normal part of the intervention process.

ESCAPE EXTINCTION PROCEDURE

Most children with selective mutism want to please others, and if manageable small goals are set and very motivating reward systems are put into place, most are quite willing to practice being brave. However, occasionally they are so used to avoiding interactions with adults that the natural inclination is to shut down and avoid brave practices. When working with these children, it can be helpful to use an escape extinction procedure. This procedure is intended to discontinue avoidance by reinforcing the child for task completion. Escape extinction should not be attempted until after a rapport is built. Generally, this intervention is used at two times:

1. If the diagnostic interview and clinical observation suggest that avoidance of speech or even participating in speech-like activities is high.
2. If progress in shaping speech through a communication ladder is stalling.

Escape extinction starts with the development of a very obtainable goal for the session, and preferably one that can be physically prompted (such as picking something up, pointing, or nodding/shaking the head). The benefit of using a goal that can be physically prompted for the first session of escape extinction is that the interventionist knows that the behavior can be completed by the end of the session, even if through prompting. The interventionist should explain that there is work to be done in the session, and that as long as the child does the work, they will get to pick out a prize and leave the office. However, if they have a hard time, that is okay—we will practice and try again. It is important to note that when using an escape extinction procedure, the child cannot be allowed to escape a task—they must stay until the behavior is completed. An interventionist should not use this procedure unless prepared to follow through until the end.

Goals can take the form of a number of times a child needs to complete the task (e.g., pointing to three pictures in the game) or a certain amount of time (e.g., five minutes of work using a sand timer). As soon as the child completes the task or works for the set amount of time, they obtain the prize and are allowed to leave (with a lot of positive praise from the interventionist). An explanation should be given to the child, such as the following:

> *"I am so excited to do our brave work today. Today, we are going to be working on point-ing, and I know that this is something you are going to do so well on. As your brave coach, I promise I will never ask you to do anything that you cannot do. I am not sure if you have ever seen a sand timer before, but here is mine. As you can see, the sand runs from the top into the bottom. We have some work to do, and as long as you are working hard the sand keeps running. As soon as all of this sand is in the bottom, you are done and get to pick a prize and go back to class. If you have trouble with the work, that is okay; I will just turn the sand timer over and we will practice, and when you are ready to try again we will turn it back up."*

If a sand timer is used, it is important that the amount of time remaining in the sand timer represents the time during which the child needs to comply, not a visual reminder of how long is left in the session. (If used incorrectly in this way, the sand timer simply acts as a visual of how much longer the child needs to avoid.) As long as a child is complying, the sand continues to run. If the child does not comply, provide one prompt (and perhaps a reminder that there is work that needs to be done so that the child can go). If the child still does not comply, stop the sand timer and prompt again, then wait a period of time to allow the child to respond/comply. During this waiting time, it is recommended that the therapist "busy himself" by either doing paperwork or picking up—obvious waiting with sustained eye contact will likely only increase the anxiety. If the child still does not comply, give the prompt again, and either physically prompt compliance (i.e., take the child's hand and point for them) or return to the last task that was successfully accomplished (i.e., take a step back on the communication ladder). After a few prompted practices or a few practices on a successful step, attempt the new step again. When the child is successful, immediately praise and restart the sand timer.

An escape extinction procedure might take place in this manner:

Therapist: *"I cannot wait to do our brave work today, and I am so excited about the great prize you are earning. Today we are going to work on pointing. I have some cards with pictures on them here, and whenever I say an animal I want you to point to your animal card that matches. I have a sand timer here; remember that as long as you are working the sand keeps running, and when the sand is all gone you get your prize and we can either just play or you can go back to class—whichever you prefer. Okay, point to the . . . cow* (make sure to give a very easy command).

Child:	Points correctly.
Therapist:	*"Great job. You knew exactly where that cow was and let me know with your pointing. Now point to the duck."*
Child:	Does not point, looks away.
Therapist:	(waits at least five seconds) *"Let's try again—point to the duck."*
Child:	Remains uncommunicative.
Therapist:	(Waits five seconds) *"Hmm . . . this must be kind of hard. I am going to stop our sand timer, and we will practice one I know you can do—point to the cow."*
Child:	Points to the cow.
Therapist:	*"Great. I love how you pointed. Okay, let's try the duck one again. Point to the duck (provides a spatial prompt by pushing the duck card forward toward the child)."*
Child:	Points to the duck.
Therapist:	*"I love how you pointed to the duck—fabulous. Let's just do it one more time to start the sand timer." Point to the duck (no spatial prompt).*
Child:	Points to the duck.
Therapist:	*"Super. We'll start the sand timer again. You are doing such great work."*

If a therapist is planning to use an escape extinction procedure, they must be careful of two things: they must have the ability to wait the child out, should the child have difficulty complying, and they must set the goal at a very attainable level with a high probability of compliance. In situations when the child has great difficulty complying, I have had to stay in the session past the allotted time, and so I generally schedule these as my last session of the day.

The goal of escape extinction is to reduce the avoidance behavior and engage the child in following your directions. After a few sessions in which the interventionist obtained compliance on a task that could be physically prompted, the goal can be changed to higher-level communicative behaviors that cannot be prompted (such as blowing air or simple sounds). As long as the child remains generally compliant with the goal behaviors, the interventionist can discontinue the escape extinction and simply practice the steps in the communication ladder. In order to maintain compliance, the interventionist must take great care not to raise the expectations too quickly or set the next step in the ladder too high. Remember: never move to the next step until the child is compliant with the current ladder step and does not appear anxious or avoidant.

CHAPTER 5

STEPS TOWARD BRAVERY (CLIMBING THE COMMUNICATION LADDER)

Long ago, a wise person made the observation that it takes a village to raise a child. It also takes a village to help a child with selective mutism, and each person has ways of being helpful and supportive.

HOW KEYWORKERS CAN HELP

"Practice makes perfect" is not just a saying; it is a way of life for kids with selective mutism. Most have spent several years practicing avoidance, and those around them have practiced reinforcing the avoidance by answering for them, not asking questions, and allowing all responses to be nonverbal communication. If you practice anything enough, you become very good at it. Thus, we MUST frequently practice being brave. Direct intervention needs to happen for at least fifteen minutes, at least three times per week (this does not count the intervention being done by the parent or outside mental health practitioner). Frequency of practice being brave is needed to counteract the frequency with which the child has practiced avoiding in the past.

After a child is building successful practices with the keyworker, either via stimulus fading or shaping procedures, it is important to begin to generalize those skills outside of the closed-office setting (e.g., practicing the use of their "brave voice" in other settings and with other people). Many children can become verbal inside a closed-office setting (especially one that becomes associated with brave talking practices) but without specific practice do not naturally generalize that speech to other people and places within the school setting.

In both the school and the clinic setting, children must work through a step-wise plan to generalize obtained speech. First, brave practices can be completed one-on-one with the keyworker, or in a small group consisting of the child, keyworker, and comfortable communication partner (e.g., parent, sibling, good friend, etc.). After consistent speech is obtained, the focus of brave practices shift to generalizing. When beginning to bring in new communication partners or practicing in new environments, it is important to change only one factor at a time—the person or the place. Changing too many factors quickly can cause a substantial increase in anxiety—one that is often not manageable for the child. Therefore, if the goal is for the child to speak to the teacher in the classroom, the first step may be for the keyworker to work with the child in the classroom while no one is present. After evoking speech in that new setting, the teacher could be faded in. Alternatively, the teacher could be first faded into the keyworker's office, where the child is used to speaking, and then the child and teacher could fade back into the classroom setting while maintaining speech.

It is beneficial to allow the child to have some control over what environments and what people will be included in the brave practices. Generally, I ask the child to use their 1-5 scale to rate how hard it would be to talk to a list of different people and in different environments in the school, and then we begin with the easiest one. Be careful not to ask the child *if* they want to talk to someone new or talk somewhere new; most will say no. Instead, you could phrase the question in a forced choice format. **"You are doing such a great job with your brave talking it's time to bring in someone new to practice with. Would you like to practice with Ms. Porter, Mr. Rodriguez, or Ms. Bunch? Could you tell me how hard it would be to use your brave voice with each of them?"**

It is important that the keyworker prepare the new communication partner for either the stimulus fading or shaping activity. An example stimulus fading sheet entitled "Fading Procedure," as well as a handout entitled "What is a Communication Ladder?" can be found on page 120. When practicing with a new communication partner or in a new environment, stimulus fading can generally be used by slowly fading a new person in to the conversation/activity or fading the speech slowly to a different setting. However, at times the child may become overwhelmed or anxious, and stimulus fading may not be possible. Shaping can also be carried out with new communication partners or in new environments. For example, the keyworker may sit with the child and a new communication partner, and work slowly up the communication ladder as a group. First, this may include all individuals practicing gestures together, blowing air, and making sounds. Eventually the group can work up to single and multiple word responses. While at first this may consist mainly of the child responding to the keyworker in front of the new communication partner, it is important that the new communication partner also become an evoker of speech by asking the child to carry out the steps of the ladder (i.e., the new communication partner should take turns giving instructions with the keyworker). If this transfer of speech does not occur, the child may speak in front of the new communication partner but never to them, and may be unable to do any "brave work" at all when the keyworker is not present.

Generalizing skills is incredibly important, since kids with selective mutism tend to be rigid and boundary-specific. Just because the child talks to the speech pathologist in her office does not mean that she/he will naturally generalize that speech to other settings, and so it must be practiced. Practice must be frequent and redundant. If a child does not see a communication partner for some time or does not regularly practice in an environment, regression can occur and the anxiety/fear surrounding that person or environment may spontaneously recur. If it does, it will be necessary to take a step back on the ladder, re-elicit speech, and then continue to practice regularly.

After a child is verbal with many people in the school setting, brave work with the keyworker could include activities that encourage the child to speak to many different people. For example, person bingo encourages speech with many individuals in a playful way. The child is given a "bingo card" which includes nine slots with common attributes or experiences, such as, "has been to Florida" or "owns a dog." The child's job is to read these attributes to different people to find "three in a row" for bingo (see page 122). The interview game encourages kids to ask several people different "favorites" questions (see page 123) in order to complete the board. Mission cards send children on independent chores that require speech, such as asking the child to deliver an envelope to the principal and letting him know that it needs to be mailed tomorrow (see page 124). Children could be given the responsibility to "interview" peers and adults in the school setting using a pre-determined list of interview questions. Having a sheet to read from and a paper/clipboard to hold in their hands also tends to reduce social anxiety.

It is also expected that successes in individualized practices by the keyworker will eventually translate to "pushing in" to the classroom setting (e.g., transition from seeing the child individually to seeing the child in a small group setting, and eventually to seeing the child in their typical classroom setting). Since the eventual goal is to help a child feel confident speaking in class to both teachers and students, the keyworker may need to practice in the classroom setting with the child, encouraging speech with other students in group activities, assisting the child in responding or initiating to the teacher, and supporting the child during oral presentations. This should only be practiced once the child is easily verbal with the keyworker in a one-on-one setting and probably only after the child has had a few successful practices one-on-one with the teacher and other peers. It is important that the keyworker take care to shape toward speech in the classroom, first starting with simpler tasks and progressing toward more difficult, anxiety-provoking speech (e.g., brave talking with the child in the corner of the classroom, then in the middle of the classroom, then in front of the class).

The highest point of the communication ladder is initiating. Whereas the eventual goal is spontaneous initiating, many children need scripted initiation or practiced initiation before they are able to spontaneously speak. For example, brave work at this level of progress may include:

- Mission cards
- Role play for an oral presentation
- Running stretches in gym class
- Presenting on a topic of interest or teaching peers a specific activity
- Initiating scripted statements to peers or teachers (see page 125)

Besides practicing in the school setting with the child and generalizing those new skills to new people and environments within the school, the keyworker's other main job is communicating with the parent, teacher, and psychologist about progress. I encourage everyone working with the child to keep a journal of practices. Progress notes can be written (this is detailed and time-consuming) or a more general log could be kept in a three-ring binder for all interventionists (keyworker, psychologist, and parent) to keep track of progress. This communication may seem like busy work, but I have seen treatment succeed or fail based solely on the communication of the team. It is vital that all main team members (i.e., keyworker, mental health professional, and parent) know what the child is successful at and/or struggling with, and what activities each member is practicing with the child. An example log sheet and blank log sheet are included on page 126.

How Mental Health Professionals Can Help

A clinical psychologist or mental health professional outside of the school is very beneficial in conducting public practices, consulting with the school, and helping to train and coach the parents on how to intervene with their children. In order to be successful, many kids need to role play the practices that they are about to take part in. Prior to conducting a public practice, be sure to do three things:

1. Have the child rate how hard they believe the practice will be (1 being very easy and 5 being very hard).

2. Role play and practice with the child. For example, if we are going to order in a restaurant, I pretend to be the clerk so that they can practice what they will order. We may even look at a menu online before leaving the office so the child can practice the exact words they are going to use. If possible, I will almost develop a "script" for the child (an over-practiced, word-for-word sequence of expected behaviors and interventions).

3. Come up with a Plan B. Everyone involved should know the contingency plan in case the chosen brave work is too hard. Some people believe that having a Plan B will encourage the child to avoid the planned interaction, but Plan B is not avoidance—it is simply a different or slightly easier option. I find that having a Plan B actually makes the child more relaxed. Just think: if you were going to do something really anxiety-provoking, wouldn't *you* want a Plan B (and C, and D. . . ...)?

Some ideas for public practices include:

- **Ordering at a restaurant.** You may find that practices need to be done both at a fast food restaurant where ordering is done at a counter, as well as at a restaurant where the waitress approaches the table.

- **Home Depot scavenger hunt.** For this task, I make a list of several items that children would not likely find on their own, and then help them ask employees where items are located.

- **Bowling.** Bowling offers the opportunity for the child to request how many games and players we want, relay shoe size, and even order a little snack at the food bar. This is also a great activity for a few children with selective mutism to do together, since they can practice talking to each other (i.e., saying things like, "it's your turn" or "great job").

- **Target, Walmart, or a similar store setting.** These locations provide many opportunities for brave speaking in one place. The security person at the front door, the optometrist, the fast food restaurant, the pharmacy, the jewelry counter, electronics department, the dressing room employee, and the floor staff are often willing to chat.

- **Nursing homes.** Children visit during lunch or dinner, and offer nursing home residents a choice of beverage at the dinner tables. Since many residents are hard of hearing, the children are naturally prompted to speak quite loudly.

- **"Safety Town" or a similar program.** Many cities or school districts offer programs which teach children safety skills. The location is set up to look like a house and children can go from room to room and try to spot the safety violations. Kids receive prizes for telling the group about all the unsafe things they observe. Some "Safety Town" programs practice fire safety, in which they pretend the house is on fire and when the fireman enters they yell, "I am over here."

- **Surveys.** Children can make up surveys asking people about their experiences, preferences, etc. and inquire with several individuals in an office setting, at the park, or in the school. For younger children, these surveys can include pictures to prompt questions.

Communication among all team members is essential. Therefore, the psychologist or outside mental health professional should set up a time for a monthly phone consult with each patient's keyworker. These consults can be very helpful in keeping track of progress, as well as brainstorming ideas to assist in reaching goals (both in the clinic and in the school). These phone consults generally consist of four parts:

How has the child been progressing in the school setting?

How has the child been progressing in the clinical setting?

What are our long-term goals for the child?

How can we modify or improve our current intervention to continue making progress toward these goals? *What else* should we be working on?

Clinical psychologists or other outside mental health professionals can also be helpful in fading in family members, family friends, or other individuals in the child's life. For example, I recently worked with a little boy who had never spoken to his babysitter. She was kind enough to attend a few sessions, with the goal of gaining speech from him. In the first session, she simply watched through a one-way mirror to observe how I interacted with him and also to observe him talking (since she had rarely seen him speak). I spent the last few minutes training her on how to fade into the next session. In the next session, I engaged him in particularly fun activities that I knew would evoke consistent speech, and she slowly faded in to the interaction. By the end of the session I was able to leave the room while he maintained speech with the babysitter. I encouraged her to practice brave talking frequently during that week, in order to generalize the speech and reduce his anxiety through practice. By the third session we were able to simply trouble-shoot some difficulties they had experienced that week, and after the third session my patient consistently talked to his babysitter.

How Parents Can Help

One of the most important jobs of a parent is encouraging social interactions. These social interactions can be divided into three main groupings:

- Extracurricular activities
- Play dates
- Interactions with extended family and family friends
- Public brave practices

As a mother of three, I realize how busy life is, and how difficult it can be to find time for the social practices. However, similar to the need for consistency and frequency of practices in the school, parents should be looking for opportunities to practice in public.

I always recommend that my patients be in extracurricular activities, as these lead to both increased self-confidence and increased social interactions with peers. When choosing an extracurricular activity, parents can consider the child's current comfort level and level of symptom severity.

Which most closely describes your child's/student's communication skills?

Level Three - These children can communicate verbally with peers and adults, although they frequently take some time to warm up. They can convey needs/wants, respond to yes/no or easy questions (at least a one-word response), and show very few physical symptoms of anxiety when placed in novel situations (e.g., sweating, freezing, poor eye contact, changes in breathing, etc.). They are willing to part from the parent to try new experiences or engage with new people.

Level Two - These children can consistently communicate needs/wants, even if it is through nonverbal means such as nodding or shaking their heads. They communicate more readily with peers, and generally have at least one friend whom they speak to easily across many different environments. They are willing to separate from parents for at least a short period of time to engage in a new activity or with new people. However, they may freeze or remain nonverbal with unknown peers and adults.

Level One - These children show significant anxiety with new adults and peers alike. They either freeze, providing very little verbal or nonverbal communication, or they are unable to engage in new tasks and activities, clinging to the parent.

If your child or student is a **Level Three,** they should be able to tolerate trying new activities, sports, or day camps, so long as they are given a "warm-up" period prior to the beginning of the activity. It is beneficial to meet with the coach or counselor individually before the activity begins, and to allow the child the time necessary to get comfortable and verbal with this individual. Furthermore, education and information should be provided to the camp, counselor, or coach, so they are aware of what SM is and how to best work with children with anxiety. Helpful information cards can be found at www.selectivemutism.org for purchase (business-size cards explaining SM and where to find more information). Examples of appropriate activities include swimming, gymnastics, soccer, girl scouts, dance, baseball, and boy scouts, among many others.

If your child is a **Level Two,** they likely can be successful in short extracurricular activities or summer activities (1-2 hours per session), particularly those that friends are attending. Group sports, summer classes on creative topics such as art or crafts, and social clubs such as Girl Scouts would be excellent opportunities to practice communicating with new peers and adults while being involved in fun activities. Education will certainly need to be provided for the adult(s) running the activity, and the child will need to be coached on nonverbal ways of communicating with adults and peers, such as nodding/shaking their head, pointing, or writing.

If your child/student is a **Level One,** it is likely that they would benefit from either participation in individual sports (e.g., swimming, running, horseback riding, etc.) or those activities and sports that do not require any communication and can easily include a parent. Parents should attempt to help the child feel comfortable at the beginning, then fade themselves out of the activity slowly, encouraging the child to engage in the activity independently.

Play dates can be rather difficult to schedule and plan. Nonetheless, play dates may be the most effective way of evoking speech with peers. Children with selective mutism often benefit from frequent play dates with "buddies" from their class. When choosing play date "buddies" from the classroom, teachers could provide suggestions of peers who would be good options. Teachers should look for peers who are slightly more advanced and can adapt to communication differences. The "buddy" should have the ability to be patient with the long latency to response that can occur in children with selective mutism. Finally, children who are not pushy and in the child's personal space, but instead are conversationally self-sufficient are good matches. When a few possible matches are determined, pair the child with SM with the possible "buddy" in a few classroom interactions and see if they are a good match. Children with SM will generally "show" us if they mesh well with the other child.

Who could be possible good matches for a buddy? What characteristics do you see that make you believe they would be a good match?

_____   _____

_____   _____

_____   _____

Once a few possible "buddies" are identified within the classroom, parents are strongly recommended to schedule play dates in their home. It is important that the "buddy" come to the home of the child with SM, as going to a new environment can inhibit communication. Some children do best when left alone to play with a peer, as comfort in their own home translates into comfort in speaking. Other children need more a more specific plan to elicit speech with friends. Generally, the intervention approach to play dates with a new child would include two main steps:

1. Parent initiates and leads interaction with child and buddy. These should be interactive play opportunities, such as arts and crafts, games that encourage speech, cooking, or pretend play (kitchen, store, stuffed animals, etc.). These could also include communicative temptations, since (especially for younger children) parents are necessary for obtaining snacks, drinks, and needed items for games/play. These are excellent opportunities to encourage speech instead of (as one parent appropriately put it) "playing the mime guessing game." As much as possible, parents should prompt the child to be verbal with them in front of the peer if not directly to the peer.

2. Once the child is verbal in the interaction (this may take some time, depending on the severity of the anxiety), the parent should slowly fade out of the interaction, first by excusing themselves for a short period of time (e.g., "I need to check on something in the oven") and then for longer periods of time, providing that speech is maintained when parents leave.

After the play date is over, it is important not to assume that speech will magically continue on from there with the buddy. The two children need to be paired as frequently as possible in the school setting, and parents need to consistently invite the buddy to play dates in their home (although the setting can change to places such as the park, pool, or school playground once comfort is established). It may be helpful to systematically plan the practice settings if possible. For example, parents hoping to transition speech from a play date into the school setting may use the following hierarchy:

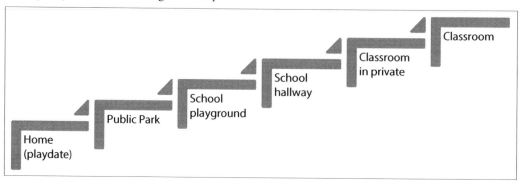

Only through repeated exposures do most children with SM become consistent communicators. Data and progress can be kept using the play date sheet on page 121.

Parents also play an important role in practicing with extended family and family friends. Generally, this means identifying family members who can practice with the child in a one-on-one setting or in a small group, using either the communication ladder or stimulus fading procedure. The best family members or family friends to focus on first are those who see the child regularly and have availability/interest in helping the child become comfortable and verbal.

For example, an aunt who can take an hour a few times a week to stop by to play board games with the child and parent while working up the communication ladder may be a great choice as a new communication partner. Alternatively, a babysitter who could come a few minutes early or stay a few minutes late and focus only on the child with selective mutism might be an appropriate new partner. While holiday parties or family dinners offer many individuals who might be willing to help, they often do not offer privacy, extended one-on-one time, or consistency of practice, and thus may not be the best settings and times in which to acquire new communication partners.

Public brave practices are very important in generalizing the child's communication to more public, novel areas. In general, it is recommended to parents that when they are out in public, the child should be responsible for social interaction of some sort at each public location. Ideas for public practices are provided in the "What Psychologists Can Do to Help" section. Although the psychologist initiates generalizing speech to the public arena, parents should continue to practice these skills with their child once the psychologist has documented headway in public. Frequently, this takes the form of "planned practices" at first. When a child is initially beginning to use their brave voice in public, the practices may take time and planning. This practice doesn't fit well into typical trips to restaurants and stores, which may be rushed, stressful, and involve distractions from siblings. Instead, planned practices are public trips with the intention and goal only of practicing being brave. For example, dad may take the child to a coffee shop alone, where he can allow the child the time and attention needed to calmly carry out the practice. Trips to the grocery store could be made with only the objective of asking where the toy section is and handing over money, not rushing to buy a cartload of food. As the child becomes more confident and consistent, practices can be carried out with less planning and more spontaneity. As a rule, the more frequent the public practice, the more quickly the child's anxiety will be reduced.

Finally, parents must take great care not to accommodate the child's anxiety. Accommodation can occur when parents change their behavior, responses, or expectations due to the child's presentation of anxiety. Some common examples of accommodation include:

- Trying to convince the child that nothing bad will happen when they talk, and they don't need to worry. This is problematic for a few reasons:
  - When others try to convince us that we shouldn't worry about something, it generally doesn't help.
  - There may be times when something undesirable does occur when the child speaks (e.g., others react with surprise)
- Speaking for the child or obtaining desired items for the child without expecting communication (this reduces any motivation for the child to speak)
- Pulling the child from extracurricular activities because they don't speak or feel anxious about attending
- Accept and excuse behavioral issues (e.g., temper tantrums, outbursts, cheating, hitting, etc.) because of an assumption that the behavior is an extension of anxiety
- Allowing the child to see our anxious behaviors without modeling coping strategies

Many of the techniques that parents do in order to help lower their child's anxiety inadvertently reinforces the anxiety. In fact, more family accommodation predicts more child anxiety and worse treatment outcomes. Children need to hear that anxiety is okay and even protective and helpful sometimes, but sometimes anxiety wears out its welcome. Children then need to be encouraged to push past their hesitations and practice being brave, even when they feel scared. Appropriate supportive statements from parents includes two parts: support/empathy for the child's experience and encouragement to move forward:

"I understand that this seems scary, but I know how brave you are—you can do it."
"This is uncomfortable but not unbearable."
"Going to soccer practice is hard but you are going to do great even though you feel afraid."

WHAT TEACHERS CAN DO TO HELP

The teacher plays an important role in helping any child feel comfortable, accepted, and genuinely liked in school. A child's self-confidence can hinge on a teacher's interactions. Teachers who do not understand the child's lack of speech may purposely exclude them (often due to a fear of increasing the child's anxiety) from classroom activities that involve speech, such as circle time. While it is generally too time-intensive for teachers to act as a keyworker, they play a vital role in the school experience of a child, and they should very quickly be integrated into the list of potential communication partners. As soon as a child is speaking to the keyworker, I typically recommend that the next person who is introduced either via stimulus fading or shaping is the teacher. However, even before that concerted effort to incorporate them begins, there are steps teachers can take to increase their interactions with the child.

Teachers should routinely encourage communication. Many teachers refrain from asking children with SM questions, because they sense it increases their anxiety. However, unless the child has an opportunity to respond, they will not develop the skills necessary to communicate with teachers. This should begin as soon as the school year is under way and rapport has been established. At that point, asking forced choice questions can provide the child with an opportunity to answer.

An important consideration when asking a question of a child with selective mutism is the ability to follow through in obtaining a response. Do not ask the question if you are not prepared to stay and obtain a response from the child, as asking a question without obtaining a response accidentally reinforces the avoidance (i.e., if the child avoids and is successful, this avoidance is more likely to be used in the future). If the child isn't able to respond to a forced-choice question, for example, the teacher should move back down the communication ladder until he/she obtains a response. An example of reversing back on the communication ladder might include:

Teacher:	*Billy, would you like pizza or a hamburger for lunch today?*
Billy:	(Silence).
Teacher:	(After at least a 5-second wait) *What do you think, Billy—pizza or hamburger?*
Billy:	(No response).
Teacher:	*Hmm . . . if you want a pizza you could say "p" and if you want a hamburger you could say "h".*
Billy:	*h*
Teacher:	*Thanks for letting me know you want a hamburger.*

Recently, I had a conversation with a patient, a young boy in the third grade. He had progressed to speaking with peers and his keyworker inside the school setting, but had not spoken to his classroom teacher. We have a very good rapport, and so I felt comfortable asking him if he knew why he had not been able to speak to her yet. He replied, "She does not care if I talk; she always tells me to write my answer or shake my head yes or no." The teacher wasn't requesting a verbal response or phrasing her questions in forced-choice format, because she did not want to make him uncomfortable, but he perceived it as ambivalence about talking. While there should be no overt pressure to talk, teachers should comment at times about their happiness in hearing the child's voice or thankfulness that the child responded to them with a gesture.

A journal can be a wonderful incentive to begin communicating with the teacher. Teachers can write down funny or interesting questions or conversation starters, and the child can respond to them at home. After this back-and-forth communication is flowing well, the journal may be transferred to a videotaped communication—the teacher videotapes him or herself asking a funny question, and the child videotapes a response. At first the videotape is viewed by the teacher alone, and then the teacher and child view it together. Soon, the proximity of videotaping may be shaped, with the teacher videotaping in one room and the child responding in another private room within the school, slowly moving closer and closer during the tapings until both are in the same room together taping. Eventually, the taping is no longer occurring, and instead the teacher is asking a question and the child is responding to it.

A similar intervention called video feed forward may prove to be effective. This self-modeling technique involves a current communication partner videotaping the child responding to simple questions, such as "favorites" questions or factual questions. Then, the teacher (or individual with whom the child does not yet communicate) videotapes himself asking these pre-determined questions. The tapes are edited to appear as if the child and novel adult are having a back-and-forth conversation. The child is asked to watch/listen to this edited tape twice a day for at least a week. After this practice period, the novel adult asks the child the same questions in a one-on-one interaction. Some research suggests that the child may speak to this person on the first trial and that behavior will generalize to other situations in which the child was previously mute (Blum, et al., 1998).

Teachers can help encourage interactions with a child at any level of communication by engaging with them, playing or interacting with them in a non-threatening way, using them as a "classroom helper," and encouraging them to communicate in nonverbal ways if necessary, such as through gestures, writing, or technology. It can be beneficial to seat a child with selective mutism next to "buddies"—children that the child already talks to, or is working on talking to, though play dates at home. A list of other possible classroom accommodations can be found in Chapter 7.

Is Intensive Treatment Right for my Child?

Recently, psychologists are noting the benefits of intensive intervention for children with selective mutism. There are many fundamental issues related to treating a child with SM in the typical psychology clinic setting. First, the clinic is not a school . . . which is the situation where the majority of the anxiety occurs. It is very difficult to help a child practice being brave enough to overcome their fear if the child is not in the environment in which the fear mainly occurs. Second, children with SM tend to have long warm-up periods, even with those people whom they see on a regular basis. It make take 15 minutes of a 45-minute session for the child to re-establish the current step on the communication ladder, and then the clinician only has a fraction of the session to make new progress up the ladder. Finally, as with many anxiety disorders, research and clinical practice suggest that elongated exposures to feared stimuli result in faster desensitization. Since evidence is clear that early intervention is of utmost importance (to short- circuit a more practiced pattern of avoidance), any time that can be saved is precious.

Consider this: a child may be able to progress five steps on the communication ladder in five weeks with the typical weekly one-hour sessions. Alternatively, with intensive intervention all five steps may be accomplished in five hours in one day. Of course we would all choose to intervene in one day. Clinical evidence (Kurtz, 2013) is demonstrating that intensive intervention not only shortens the overall tie of intervention required but also the hours of brave practices necessary.

There are many different options for "intensive" intervention.

- **Intensive treatment sessions in the psychologist's office.** This reduces warm-up time and allows for possibly faster progression toward speech. The child's developmental ability to maintain energy/focus needs to be considered in determining the length of a session, and parent finances may be a consideration, as most insurance companies will not pay for more than "treatment as usual"—45-minute sessions once per week.

- **Intensive treatment sessions in the school setting, conducted either by the keyworker or the psychologist.** This reduces warm-up time, allows for likely faster progression toward speech, and may reduce the need for a long-term pull-out program (and the potential disruptions to the child's schedule that individual intervention involves). The cons of intensive interventions in the school include disruptions to the child's school schedule for a short period of time while the intensive intervention is occurring, as well as the complexity of scheduling the psychologist or keyworker to be available for several days in a row.

  Intensive in-school intervention can occur over the span of one week, with approximately twenty hours of treatment within the school setting. The intervention utilizes stimulus fading and/or shaping, with the goal of increasing the number of communication partners and environments in which the child speaks. Additionally, school staff are trained in the behavioral intervention (so that appropriate treatment can continue after the week of intensive intervention, and an individualized accommodation plan is drafted.

  Initial observations suggest that intensive in-school intervention may be more effective than weekly treatment as usual. Experts at Thriving Minds Behavioral Health offer intensive in-school interventions nationally and internationally. Visit www. selectivemutismtreatment.com for more information.

- **Intensive group treatment in a school-like setting. Summer camps are available nationally for children with selective mutism.** The goal of these camps is to simulate a classroom setting and allow the child to practice their brave behaviors with support. Camps such as Confident Kids Camp© (www.confidentkidscamp.com) are organized to expose children to the anxiety-provoking situations of school, such as responding to the teacher's questions, show-and-tell and oral presentations, and group projects. Each child is paired with their own "camp counselor"—a trained therapist who provides individualized support throughout the week. Camps provide a child with the ability to practice brave talking right before the start of a new school year, and research is demonstrating a large increase in speech during the week of camp and maintenance of those gains into the new school year. Camps provide intensive practice with no real disruption to the child's schedule, and allow parents and children to meet other families also struggling with selective mutism.

Research has found that Confident Kids Camp is effective in increasing overall speech and that these gains carry over into the school setting following camp. Specifically, Confident Kids Camp leads to a significant decline in the symptoms of selective mutism, an increase in the use of phrases, sentences, and responses during the time of camp and a significant decline in anxiety during the week of camp (Schultz, 2014). Other nationwide camps with similar behaviorally-based curriculums are finding comparable gains.

CHAPTER 6

BARRIERS TO GREATNESS
(HOW TO AVOID PITFALLS)

WHAT IF THEY DON'T ANSWER?

This is the consistent question of parents, teachers, and everyone committed to helping a child with selective mutism. First, here are some tips to consider that might help increase the likelihood of obtaining a response.

1. Generally, it is easier for the child to speak to familiar people rather than unfamiliar people, particularly those with whom the child already has an established rapport. The exception to this rule is individuals who have become "contaminated." Contaminated individuals could be people who have known the child for quite some time, but to whom the child has never spoken. The longer a child knows someone and does not talk to them, the greater the chance of contamination. This is likely because these people know the child as "the kid who does not talk," and perhaps the child is very anxious about the response of that person when they do finally speak. For this reason, some children have less anxiety about speaking to novel people who don't know them as these people have no preconceived notions and will not express surprise if they do talk. Contamination does not mean that the child will never speak to the individual, but it may be much more difficult to evoke speech.

2. Women tend to be easier to talk to than men (this is not always true, but true in general).

3. The smaller the audience, the easier it is for the child to speak. If the child freezes and is unable to respond, consider the size of their perceived "audience"—who is watching? Who might be able to overhear? You may need to move to a more private location or reduce the number of people in the environment if the child is unable to respond.

4. Consider the type of response you are trying to evoke. Is it an open-ended response? Is it particularly emotionally-laden? Is it very personal? Does it require a great verbal demand from the child? Avoid thought-provoking or difficult questions—begin with general knowledge or concrete questions. The goal is to build the child's comfort level with speaking, not challenge their knowledge. Often, the prompt to speak can be made easier simply by switching to a forced-choice question or asking a new question altogether.

5. Is it possible that you did not provide the "correct" answer in your forced-choice question? If you asked a child, "What do you want for lunch—a sandwich or a hotdog?" and the

child wants a hamburger, they may not respond. The choices may need to be altered to allow for other answers, such as, "What do you want for lunch—a sandwich, a hotdog, or something different?"

6. Sustained and intense eye contact and attention can reduce the likelihood that kids respond or engage with others. Most people (even those with no social anxiety at all) can only maintain eye contact for around three seconds before it becomes uncomfortable, and children with selective mutism tend to become overwhelmed by sustained eye contact. Therefore, it is best to make minimal eye contact when playing, and perhaps sit next to the child instead of across from them in play. At times, even turning your back or turning to the side can help evoke more verbalizations, as it is an obvious way of taking direct attention off of the child.

7. If the child believes that they are being tested or graded, they may be more inhibited or anxious.

If you are taking care to make the situation as easy for the child as possible, but the child still has difficulty responding, there are several options:

- **Wait 5 seconds and ask again.** <u>This should be the first step taken whenever a child does not respond.</u>

- **Ask differently.** Change the way in which you ask the question by rephrasing your forced choice question or making the question easier.

- **Reduce expectations.** Take a step back on the communication ladder. For example, if you are asking a question that requires a one-word response, and the child is unable to answer, revert to sounds or sound combinations. If they are unable to make sounds, move back to mouthing or blowing air. Try to refrain from moving all the way back to nonverbal communication once a child is verbal, but obtaining nonverbal communication is better than total avoidance.

- **Move to a different area or do a "sidebar."** If you feel that the child is reacting to their environment, it may be necessary to move to a quieter place or a place with fewer people around. If you feel that the child is struggling in speaking to a new person, a sidebar could be used. A sidebar simply means moving away from others for a moment, allowing the child to regain their composure, and practicing the question before returning to the original interaction. For example, if the child is practicing answering questions with the teacher but freezes, the keyworker could pull the child aside, give them a moment to calm down, and ask the question again privately. Once the child is able to answer the keyworker privately, both could return to the teacher, and the teacher could ask the child again. If the child is still unable to answer the teacher directly, answering the keyworker in front of the teacher may be a good step in shaping toward talking directly to the teacher.

Once the child is responding verbally to the teacher (or any other adult), the response chain should be followed.

Response Chaining for Selective Mutism

```
                    ┌─────────────────────┐
                    │   Adult Question    │
                    │   (Forced Choice)   │
                    └─────────────────────┘
           ┌───────────────┼───────────────┐
           ▼               ▼               ▼
   ┌──────────────┐ ┌──────────────┐ ┌──────────────┐
   │   Verbal     │ │ No response  │ │  Nonverbal   │
   │  response    │ │              │ │  response    │
   └──────────────┘ └──────────────┘ └──────────────┘
           │               │               │
           ▼               ▼               ▼
   ┌──────────────┐ ┌──────────────┐ ┌──────────────┐
   │   Labeled    │ │ Wait 5       │ │ Probe for    │
   │   praise     │ │ seconds,     │ │ verbal       │
   │              │ │ repeat       │ │ response     │
   │              │ │ question     │ │              │
   └──────────────┘ └──────────────┘ └──────────────┘
```

Adult Question (Forced Choice) →

- **Verbal response** → **Labeled praise**
- **No response** → **Wait 5 seconds, repeat question**
- **Nonverbal response** → **Probe for verbal response**

Wait 5 seconds, repeat question / Probe for verbal response →

- **Verbal response** → **Labeled praise**
- **No response or nonverbal response** → **Wait 5 seconds; reduce expectations (take a step back on the ladder)**

HOW TO COMBAT "THE WHISPERER" (AND OTHER TRANSITIONAL SPEECH)

When children with selective mutism transition into speech after not speaking in public for some time, it is not uncommon for them to use a "transitional voice." This can take many forms:

- Whispering
- "Baby talk" or an immature speech pattern
- Muffled or unintelligible speech
- Altered speech (e.g., strange accents, staccato speech, etc.)

These transitional voices are likely a protective coping strategy, allowing the child to begin speaking without others truly hearing their real voice. If possible, caregivers should try to ensure that these transitional speech patterns are not reinforced from the very beginning. It is especially important to avoid reinforcing a whispered response, because whispering tends to be maintained if accepted from the start. In order to reduce whispering, I typically ask children at the initial step of the intervention to use their real voice. For example, when transitioning from voiceless sounds to voiced sounds on the communication ladder, the sounds that are reinforced are real sounds—sounds that make the child's larynx rumble. If the child is not using his or her larynx to make those sounds, they are not truly making voiced sounds. Generally, I recommend continuing at that step in the ladder until the sounds are voiced.

If a child is already whispering at the beginning of treatment, some techniques that have been helpful to increase volume are simple verbal prompts ("I couldn't hear you—please use your real voice"), gestural prompts (cupping an ear), setting volume as the goal of the session (an app on iPhones® called "Decibel" provides a decibel feedback of the loudness of the child's voice volume—a goal could be saying ten words at 50 decibels), playing fun games or activities that require a louder voice ("Talking Tom" apps on the iPad or iPhone are helpful for increasing speech, as they rarely mimic whispered sounds), or moving back down the ladder to voiced sounds again, perhaps even working on non-word voiced sounds such as environmental noises, throat clearing, coughing, laughing, or animal sounds. Alternatively, if the intervention is stimulus fading, fading should only occur when the child is using a regular voice. If the child is whispering or using altered speech, the parent should continue working, prompting, and reinforcing regular speech before a novel individual begins the fading procedure.

Acting silly and humorous can help reduce the child's anxiety and encourage speech. For example, Dr. Jacqueline Hood uses the game Hungry Hungry Hippos™ to elicit louder speech (J. Hood, personal communication, February 26, 2014). First, a practical explanation should be given prior to moving into the exercise. "This is why this game is helpful—it can help us use a louder and stronger brave voice, and here's a way to make it fun."

Start by having the child come up with silly sentences that they either think of or write down, and the interventionist should create some of their own (e.g., "The flying penguin is wearing a polka-dot bathing suit"). The goal is to say the silly sentence while playing Hungry Hungry Hippos in a loud enough voice to be understood. First, the interventionist says the sentence in a soft voice, then the child's job is to say, "Louder." when they cannot hear, until the interventionist reaches a volume loud enough to be heard over the game. The child then repeats the silly sentence in a voice loud enough to hear. When the balls are eaten, play stops and the child must repeat the sentence in a "medium" voice (no Hippo eating sounds to hide behind) to be sure he/she "really heard." Next, the child takes a turn to say one of their sentences while playing until he/she can be understood. When the child and interventionist are both using a loud and clear voice, other individuals can be faded slowly into the play (Hood, 2014).

There are times when accepting whispering may be the only way to start making progress. If as an interventionist you feel that the child is capable of increasing the amount of speech, but not yet the volume of speech, and you have tried increasing volume with only a reduction in the amount of speech as an outcome, whispering may have to be acceptable for a time. In my work with children who have SM, about 25% of those whom I have treated fall into this category. With these kids I may choose to set my first goal to increase speech and then later correct the volume of speech.

WHAT IF THEY DON'T *WANT* TO TALK?

Nothing halts treatment like a child who does not want to talk. This lack of motivation to change occurs most frequently in older children and adolescents and less so in young children. I have worked with many kids who feel they cannot talk (hopelessness) or don't know how to get started (lack of a good intervention), but these concerns are much easier to address because I (and now you.) know the interventions that work and can start them down the road to success.

However, some children don't see the benefit of speaking; everything they want and need has been provided for them without the requirement of speech and without the perceived risk inherent in engaging in verbal behavior (e.g., evaluation, providing an incorrect response, being judged). When children are not actively participating in the intervention, we need to ask ourselves if they have any motivators to communicate verbally, or if nonverbal communication meets their every need. I recently heard a joke about a 6-year-old boy who never spoke to his mother. One day during breakfast, he broke his silence by saying, "This toast is burned." His mother was stunned and asked why he had not spoken before. He paused, considering, and stated, "Well, because everything has been all right up until now." We generally do not learn new skills or attempt difficult tasks unless there is a *need* to make change and that change is perceived as *achievable*.

But what if the child voices an overt desire not to talk? At times, a psychological technique called motivational interviewing (Rollnick, 1995) can be helpful in increasing internal motivation to make change. Motivational interviewing is a therapeutic approach that aims to identify and later resolve the ambivalence children and adolescents feel about changing their behavior. Parents and/or adults with excellent rapport and open communication may be the best people to utilize this technique, since it does require higher level, back-and-forth conversation.

Change is not feasible if the child does not want to change. It is important that prior to attempting motivational interviewing techniques, you assess the child's readiness to change and confidence in his or her ability to make this change. This can be assessed by a readiness ruler or a visual aid numbered 1-5 where the child can mark his or her current readiness to change. **When you think about getting braver and using your voice more at school and in public, are you not prepared to change, already changing or somewhere in the middle?**

Not prepared to change 1	A little ready to change 2	Somewhat ready to change 3	Very ready to change 4	Already Changing 5

Readiness to change can also be assessed more subtly, through the recognition of "change talk." The child may use statements that signify desire, ability, reasons, need or commitment to change. By recognizing the specific statements that signify these stages in the change process, you can tailor your techniques to where the child is in terms of his or her readiness to change.

Desire
(I would like to, I wish)
Ability
(I think I could, I am able, I can)
Reasons
(I know I would feel better, I would be able to ___)
Need
(I should, I have to)
Commitment
(Low level: I hope to, I will try to, I plan to)
(High level: I will, I am going to, I promise)

So how does one motivate a child with selective mutism to speak? The following are specific techniques that can be used to evoke "change talk."

1. List of pros and cons (benefits/costs) for and against using their brave voice more in school and in public.

2. Looking forward—the child thinks about his or her hopes for the future, how he or she would like things to be different, and what would be the best results he or she could imagine if the change is made.

3. Exploring goals—highlight the difference between the child's current situation and his or her ideal life. By pointing out this discrepancy, children are more likely to decide that they would like to move toward their ideal life by changing their behavior.

During this discussion, it is best to use open-ended questions, so the child is able to explore their reasoning in a more meaningful way than by answering a "yes/no" question. Open-ended questions may not be feasible in all cases depending on the child's comfort in answering such questions, and is an additional reason that parents may make the best conversational partners for motivational interviewing. Another way to frame this discussion is to have the child in the position of arguing *for* change and *against* remaining the same. This can be especially helpful, because people are more likely to internalize and act upon their own reasoning. In short, the aim is not to inundate the child with all the reasons you think they should change but to guide them to this realization (Lynas, 2012).

Some specific questions that could be included are:

1. **Ask about the positive aspects of the problem behavior (e.g. maintaining the mutism in school and in public).**
    *   What are some of the good things about _____?
    *   Summarize the positives.

2. **Ask about the negative aspects of the target behavior:**
    *   Can you tell me about the downside?
    *   What are some things you are not so happy about?
    *   Summarize the negatives.

3. **Explore life goals and values.** These goals will be the pivotal point against which cost and benefits are weighed.

   - What sort of person would you like to be? What do you want to do when you grow up?
   - If things worked out in the best possible way for you, what would you be doing a year from now?
   - Use affirmations to support "positive" goals and values.

4. **Restate the dilemma or ambivalence and then ask for a decision.**

   - **If the decision is positive, the next step is goal setting—Use SMART goals** (specific, meaningful, assessable, realistic, timed)
   - What will be your next step?
   - What will you do in the next one or two days?
   - On a scale of 1 to 10 what are the chances that you will do your next step? (anything under 7 and their goal may need to be more achievable)

5. **If there is no decision or the decision is to continue the behavior.**

   - If no decision, empathize with difficulty of ambivalence.
   - Ask if there is something else which would help them make a decision.
   - Ask if they have a plan to manage not making a decision.
   - If the decision is to continue the behavior, go back to explore the ambivalence.

*Adapted from the work of Rollnick, 1995.

Throughout the discussion, it is important to underscore the child's strengths, particularly when they are discouraged by previously failed attempts to change. It is also important to convey that you understand what the child is saying by reflecting their statements. In fact, reflections allow the parent to further emphasize the negatives of remaining the same and the positives of changing. As noted in the PRIDE skills section, reflections are a restatement of information the child communicates. Below are examples of reflections:

Child statement:	"I am scared that if I talk, everyone will look at me."
Reflection:	"You are interested in talking, but worry that if you do, people might look at you."
Child statement:	"I guess talking would make school easier, because I could ask the teacher questions."
Reflection:	"So there are positives to talking at school that would make school a lot easier, like asking the teacher questions if you don't understand."

FACING RESISTANCE

Change can be a scary process. Despite the negative outcomes associated with current behavior, staying in one's old ways can be more comfortable than changing. Therefore, throughout the discussion the child might express various types of resistance to the process. This might include arguing and other forms of avoidance of change, like interrupting, inattention, side-tracking, etc. In motivational interviewing, resistance is not directly addressed. Instead, acknowledge the emotion the child is presenting. Tie this into a statement about their ambivalence. For example, you might say something like: "So you said you want to talk more at school, but it also seems like you are worried that other people will take special notice of you if you talk, and you don't want that to happen." Simpler reflections can also be used to clarify that you are on the same page as the child, that you understand their reluctance. This will likely improve the rapport with the child—everyone prefers feeling understood, including children and adolescents.

SELECTIVE MUTISM "DON'TS"

Many school staff, professionals, and parents try to intervene effectively and yet make mistakes along the way (as do I—we are human). This book has provided many ideas or actions that interventionists and parents "should" do to assist a child with selective mutism, but it is always good to know exactly what NOT to do.

Here is a "Don'ts" cheat sheet to help.

- **Don't provide too many escape routes or avoidance techniques for kids.** While we cannot hurry them along too much, we also don't want to provide too many crutches. Teaching sign language, using assistive technology, or only asking questions that allow a nonverbal response may reduce the motivation to speak—why would the child talk if they can convey every want, need, and thought nonverbally? We must take care to begin to reduce our rescuing and instead begin encouraging the child to use verbalizations to get needs met. That is not to say that the expectation should immediately be that the child must verbalize to obtain what they want, but that eventually 'talking gets the good stuff' and we become much less responsive to nonverbal communication.

- **Don't accidentally reinforce.** Reinforcement should be given for the current step on the ladder and ones higher, and at some point nonverbal responses should no longer be accepted or rewarded. For example, if I take a child to order a cookie at a coffee shop, and despite all of our practice and planning, they just simply are not able to order, do I order the cookie for them? *No.* It breaks my heart a little to walk out of that store with no cookie, but I convey to them, "I know you worked really hard, and we will try again next time."

- **Don't mind-read. Most of us have become quite good at knowing what the child with selective mutism wants before they even indicate it.** For example, I recently discovered that the mother of a teenage patient with SM knew what her daughter wanted from all of her favorite restaurants, and automatically ordered for her without even asking the daughter or suggesting the daughter play a role in ordering her own food. I joke in workshops by saying that I become very "dumb" when I work with kids with selective mutism. I suddenly forget and cannot understand what they want unless they say it, and cannot hear well unless they speak up. Kids need for us to begin reducing our automatic knowledge of what they want, and begin asking them to take responsibility for indicating, even nonverbally, their choices, needs, and desires.

- **Take great care not to be critical or discouraging.** I realize that working with these children is sometimes frustrating, discouraging, and slow. However, critical comments to or about them will not help. These children do not "just need a good spanking." Trying to force them to talk will not work. Do not do it.

- **Don't allow the child to see your anxiety or frustration.** While both of those emotions are normal when working with children with selective mutism, they are in no way helpful to the child. Keep them to yourself. This is not about *our* goals and where *we* think they should be—it is about *their* goals and *their* progress.

- **When shaping using a communication ladder, be very careful about jumping steps on the ladder.** There is a reason that slow, steady progression works—because it is within the ability level of the child and does not elevate them to an unmanageable level of anxiety. If you jump steps, you may place them in a position of being unable to perform. If in doubt, always go slow or move back one step on the ladder.

- **Don't get greedy.** We are all encouraged by seeing a child's progress, and we often want to promote and maintain that progress as much as possible. Therefore, we sometimes ask kids to push themselves farther and faster than previously agreed upon. If I had agreed with a child that we were going to play one game of Person Bingo, I should offer to end the game after one round regardless of how the child is doing. If the child wants to continue the game, great. If I request that they continue playing longer than previously agreed upon, I become unpredictable and untrustworthy in their eyes.

- **Don't say, "Don't worry—no one will hear you."** At times, I am working with children in my office, and the children are obviously concerned about someone overhearing them speak (i.e., they are glancing around, lowering their voices, and moving closer to me). I know that the others in the office are not listening, and probably could not overhear them even if they were listening, but I must not convey that to the child. The entire goal of the treatment is to desensitize them to people hearing their voices, so these statements are not helpful. Telling them not to worry because that specific person will not hear them communicates the same message as if I told a child who was afraid of dogs, "Don't worry—that one will not bite you." The underlying message? This one might not bite, but the next one could.

- **Not practicing brave talking enough leads directly to . . . not brave talking enough.** The child must practice frequently and repeatedly to be successful and for those gains to be maintained. We would not expect for a child to learn to read a word with one presentation and no continued practice. Practice must be maintained and consistent.

- **Don't set the bar too high.** As adults, we tend to want quick change, quick turnaround, and quick outcomes. However, we must work at the child's speed and comfort level. If you had a fear and were trying hard to face it, I am certain you would want others supporting you, standing beside you and cheering you on, not nagging at you to "hurry up and get over it" (the underlying message when we are asking a child to change quickly). Desensitization takes time and patience.

- **Don't ask open-ended questions.** These are typically difficult for children with SM to answer. Instead, try to phrase questions as forced-choice.

- **Don't bombard them with questions.** At times, parents can get nervous and embarrassed, and react to that anxiety by asking dozens of questions in rapid-fire succession. Ask a question, provide a pause for the child to respond (at least 5 seconds.) and if they don't respond ask the same question again or rephrase the same question.

- **Don't focus on polite words . . . yet.** Many parents complain that the hardest words for their children to say are polite words such as "sorry," "thank you," "please," and "excuse me." Research has not found an answer for this phenomenon yet, but it is possible that children have "over-practiced" avoiding these words. Parents have attempted over and over to encourage their child to say "please" or "thank you" in public, and the child has therefore garnered a lot of practice avoiding saying these phrases. In the beginning of treatment, I ask parents not to prompt their child to greet me in the waiting room, say goodbye to me after the appointment, or thank me after receiving their toy. We will work on these phrases later and, until we do, prompting them generally only sets us up for failure.

- **Don't worry about having your child use proper names when speaking to friends and family.** Another interesting anomaly about children with selective mutism is that they are often hesitant or even unable/unwilling to use proper names, even if they know the names well. Again, this is something that can be the focus later in the intervention, but should be put aside at the start.

- **Don't make a lot of eye contact.** As noted before, this can increase anxiety. Generally, as the child becomes more comfortable with you and others eye contact naturally follows.

- **Don't let your anxiety get in the way.** It is okay for a child to struggle a little, and it has to be okay for them to be a little uncomfortable. As noted before, individual growth does not come as a result of doing only things that are easy and comfortable. Try to manage your own anxiety privately.

COACHING OTHERS TO BE HELPFUL

- It is the holiday season, and dreaded Aunt Nancy is going to be at the family Christmas party. Not only does she not help Isaac speak, but her behavior actually makes Isaac's anxiety worse. Every year it is the same interaction—she runs up to Isaac, asks him several questions in front of a big group of family members, and asks Isaac's parents why he will not talk.

- Ben is a child in a large extended family. Family members consistently tell Ben's parents that he will grow out of his silence, and that there is no reason to work on it because nothing is really wrong with him. Family members tend to either ignore him or just ask him yes/no questions, and don't seem concerned that he does not talk to them.

- The coach at soccer practice alerts Baylee's parents that she needs to start talking or she will be thrown off the team. After all, she probably just needs a stern talk and some consequences.

Do any of these examples sound like your child, or the child you are working with? The first step is educating others on selective mutism; many people act inappropriately because they simply do not understand. Encourage others in the child's life to be accepting, warm, and caring toward the child. Mutism is not a behavior that the child chose, nor is it born of oppositionality. Providing a caring, accepting, and nurturing environment is of upmost importance. Ask other adults to allow the child warm-up time without questions or a lot of direct speech. Encourage the adults to play with them, smile at them, and have fun with them. Buy books on selective mutism and loan them out to teachers, grandparents, and soccer coaches. Request close family and friends consider meeting one-on-one with the child using a communication ladder or stimulus fading procedure to increase speech (with the help and training of either a knowledgeable parent or a mental health professional). A handout that could be given to the adults in the child's life is provided on page 128. Write up a small letter about your child, the wonderful strengths that he or she exhibits, and the best ways to interact with them. An example letter might include:

Dear Family and Friends,

You may have noticed that it is difficult for _____ to speak to you, and sometimes even for him/her to respond to you at all. _____ has an anxiety disorder called selective mutism—while he/she can speak comfortably at home or with immediate family, he/she is unable to speak in other social situations (especially at school and in public). This behavior is not normal shyness, stubbornness, or defiance; instead, it is a fear of other people hearing his/her voice. It does not develop from abuse, bad parenting, or trauma—it has a biological basis like many anxiety disorders. At home or when fully comfortable, _____ is bright, funny, and engaging.

I am so happy that you are part of _____'s life, and the good news is that there are things you can do to help.

- *Be warm and caring toward _____. Please love and accept him/her unconditionally. Know that although he/she cannot yet, he/she wants to speak to you.*

- *Give _____ time to warm up when you first see him/her. It may take _____ longer to warm up than other children, and during this time it is helpful not to ask direct questions. Instead, feel free to play with _____, comment on what he/she is doing, and give quiet praise.*

- *When you have time, playing or interacting with _____ in a one-on-one basis is likely the best way to relate to him/her . . . and it is in these moments that he/she might be more likely to talk to you.*

- *After the warm-up time, look for opportunities to ask him/her a question. Give _____ 5 seconds to think about his/her responses and build up his/her bravery. _____ is not ignoring you or being rude—he/she is simply building up confidence.*

- *You can reword questions if _____ is not able to answer you. For example, you could ask the question as a forced choice question ("Which snack do you want—an apple or an orange?") or a yes/no question ("Do you want an apple?") instead of an open-ended question ("What do you want to eat?").*

- *If _____ does talk, please don't make a big deal out of it.*

- *Please don't try to bribe _____ to talk. It usually does not work and can put a lot of extra pressure on him/her.*

It is not always easy when others don't understand _____'s diagnosis, and you could be a huge support to us as parents by:

- *Understanding that this condition is not due to bad parenting—we are doing the best we can. It cannot be changed by discipline or harsh correcting, which is why we don't use those strategies.*

- *Understanding that generally kids don't grow out of it, which is why we are seeking professional help for the selective mutism. Please support us in that.*

- *Do say that you care and ask how you can help.*

_____ is currently involved in therapy to learn how to be braver and stronger, and is working hard.

If you would like to learn more about selective mutism, visit www.selectivemutism.org. Thank you for caring about _____.

Sincerely,

Peers also need instruction about the child with SM and reminders of how to help the child. Generally, I do not recommend excusing the child from class and having a discussion about selective mutism. I can almost guarantee that the moment the child returns to class, someone will let them know about the discussion and they will be mortified. Instead, when a peer asks why the child does not speak, or when the peer speaks for the child with selective mutism, it is helpful to pull them aside privately and explain: "Justin does talk at home, and he will talk here when he is ready. Until then, it is helpful if you play with him and are kind to him, but please don't answer for him or ask why he does not talk." If the child with SM is willing, encourage them to write a letter to peers at school explaining their diagnosis, how it impacts them, and what peers can do to help. An example letter for peers might include:

Dear Friend,

My name is Casey. I like animals, skiing, reading, and playing with my cat Ginger. I especially love riding my bike.

I also love to talk and love to make friends. But when I am at school, at birthday parties, or when I meet someone new, I get very nervous and cannot talk. I feel like the words get stuck in my throat. This is not because I do not like you. I have an anxiety disorder called selective mutism which sometimes makes it hard for me to talk to you. Here are some things you can do to help:

- When you first see me, don't come running up to me and try to get me to talk. This only makes me more nervous.
- Please say hello to me but understand that it may take me time to respond to you. If I don't answer, give me some time. If I wave and do not say "hello," please do not think I am rude. I may feel very nervous and the words may be stuck.
- If you come over to see me at my house, maybe we could play with my Barbies® or videogames on my dad's iPad. This helps me to get to know you better and feel more comfortable. As I get more comfortable, I may point or nod to you when you ask me a question. Or, I may tell my mom or dad something, and they can then tell you.
- I like it when you joke and have fun with me like you would with anyone else in the room.
- Please DO ask me questions, but ask me choice questions or yes/no questions rather than questions that I need to explain an answer to you. And, give me time to answer. You may have to ask the question again. It is fine and this helps me. I may point, nod, or write to you. Then, as I get comfortable, I may tell someone in front of you or answer you directly.

Thank you for taking the time to read this. I am trying hard to get braver but it takes some time and I need other people to help me. At first I am working on non-talking ways to answer you, so I may nod, point or maybe write you a note. This helps me get comfortable using my words around you. Thank you for understanding.

Casey

DO REGRESSIONS OCCUR?

Minor regressions occur on an everyday basis for kids with selective mutism. As mentioned previously, kids with selective mutism generally require a longer-than-typical warm-up time, and therefore it is very common for a child who is already verbal with me to need a few minutes to re-establish speech when I see them again. Each day of school may require a short period of time in the morning to return to previous functioning.

The longer the break in practices or exposure, the larger the possible regression. The summer break is often a time of regression for the child, since there are generally few social demands or school-related exposures during these months, and thus very little brave practicing. Likewise, if a child has not seen a family member or friend for quite some time, there may be a significant regression. For instance, if a child only sees grandparents once a year, then each year they may revert back to mutism when interacting with the grandparents again.

Generally, interventions can help reduce or eliminate these regressions. There are several options for brave practices during the summer, including Skyping with grandparents regularly, summer visits by the teacher or keyworker, or preparing for school by attending a summer camp. Occasionally, a large change or upsetting event can result in a more obvious and long-standing regression. Puberty, changing to a new school (particularly moving from elementary school to middle school, where there are many teachers and the demand for independence is high), and a socially embarrassing event can set a child back. If that occurs, revisiting behavioral treatment may be necessary.

CHAPTER 7

INTEGRATING TREATMENT INTO THE SCHOOL ENVIRONMENT

The anxiety and lack of speech associated with selective mutism frequently results in academic limitations for children with SM. Many children cannot ask clarifying questions, provide an oral presentation, participate effectively and fully in a group project, request to use the restroom, make and keep social relationships, or ask for help if injured. These limitations suggest the need for a special education plan such as a Section 504 Plan or an Individualized Education Plan (IEP).

A Section 504 Plan is an adaptations and modifications plan specifically intended for the classroom setting (mandated by the civil rights law establishing the rights of individuals with disabilities). This document provides the child with in-classroom accommodations, but no direct, individualized services (i.e., the child will not obtain one-on-one sessions with the keyworker). The Section 504 Plan may be an appropriate fit for students with mild selective mutism who do not need specialized services but instead may need minor accommodations for specific situations, such as oral presentations.

Alternatively, an Individualized Education Plan (IEP) is a specialized program within the school setting designed to meet a child's specific needs (mandated by the Individuals with Disabilities Education Act—IDEA). A child must qualify for an IEP via federal regulations and, if a disability is identified that meets federal criteria, the plan identifies accommodations and interventions both in the classroom and through related service providers in the school. Simply put, an IEP is the legal document that opens the doors to both in-classroom accommodations (e.g., preferential seating next to communication partners, alternative ways to do oral presentations, etc.) as well as direct, individualized services (e.g., one-on-one "brave work" with the keyworker in the school).

An IEP is generally necessary, since most children with selective mutism need to begin their "brave work" in a one-on-one setting with an interventionist. In order to qualify for an IEP, a child needs more than just a diagnosis of a disability. There must be evidence that the disability has an adverse effect on the child's educational progress. This is the sticking point for many schools who have children with selective mutism—most children with SM are smart, capable, and manage to do well academically despite the lack of speech.

Some schools are hesitant to provide special education planning or intervention to children with selective mutism if there is not an overt negative academic impact. If the school is willing to provide intervention on a regular basis without an official special education plan, this might be a wonderful first step. Parents and school professionals should keep logs of the response to intervention as well as the consistency of the intervention (assuming that the response) is consistently meeting goals and the consistency is as promised, an official plan may not be necessary.

If, however, a school is unwilling or unable to provide consistent intervention in a one-on-one format, a special education plan may be necessary to legally ascertain services. The first step toward requesting special education services is through a *written letter* to the school. A sample letter is provided on page 130. Parents should highlight their specific concerns, particularly the ways that the child is impacted academically by selective mutism. Common impacts of selective mutism include:

- Difficulty or inability to participate in group work or group projects
- Difficulty or inability to participate in oral presentations
- Inability to ask clarifying questions or request help from the teacher
- Inability, difficulty, or inaccuracy in participating in the academic assessment process
- Difficulty or inability to benefit from social learning opportunities
- Difficulty or inability to learn and practice collaborative problem-solving techniques
- Difficulty or inability to engage the assistance of others when necessary for educational, health or safety reasons
- Inability to learn through repetition of concepts by teaching others
- Inappropriate types of behaviors or feelings under normal circumstances

The main goal of the educational institution is to prepare a child for higher-level education or a vocation following graduation. If a child does not speak, how will he or she be successfully prepared for college or a vocation?

Once a written letter has been delivered, the school will begin determining if a child meets the criteria for special education services. To make this determination, a number of requirements must be fulfilled, including documented interventions and the child's response (or lack of response) and psycho-educational evaluation which may consist of those evaluative tools listed in Chapter 3. This information is taken together to make the determination of whether or not a child qualifies for Special Education. In order to obtain an IEP, the child must meet certain criteria for a designation of services. The most common designations to obtain services for children with selective mutism are:

Speech/Language Impairment (SLI) or Communication Impairment (CI)—defined as a communication disorder that adversely affects a child's learning. A language disorder "may be characterized by difficulty in understanding and producing language, including word meanings (semantics), the components of words (morphology), the components of sentences (syntax), or the conventions of conversation (pragmatics)" (Head Start, 2006). Children with selective mutism may have primary disabilities in speech (including semantics, articulation, and fluency), but also have social pragmatic speech weaknesses (the ability to utilize speech effectively in social situations).

Other Health Impaired (OHI)—defined as a child who has a chronic or acute health condition that limits alertness to the educational environment due to either limited strength, vitality, and alertness or heightened alertness to the surrounding environment. Like other designations, this issue must impair academic performance (Grice, 2002).

Emotional Disturbance/Disability (ED)—defined as a child whose education is impacted by one or more of the following:

- An inability to learn that cannot be explained by intellectual, sensory, or health factors.
- An inability to build or maintain satisfactory interpersonal relationships with peers and teachers.
- Inappropriate types of behavior or feelings under normal circumstances.
- A general pervasive mood of unhappiness or depression.
- A tendency to develop physical symptoms or fears associated with personal or school problems.

While all of these designations have different requirements, they all simply open the door to services for the child. Once that door to services is opened, the specific services and interventions are determined by the individual need of the child, not the designation itself. Many practitioners feel that speech/language impairment and other health impaired are the most fitting designations, but in the end the issue that matters the most is not how we label it, but that the child with selective mutism obtains the services they require. For more information on the steps of the IEP process, what to expect from the meeting, and how to successfully advocate for your child, Wrights Law (www.wrightslaw.com) has a multitude of resources. This website is not specific to selective mutism, but can be extremely helpful for parents navigating the special education process.

It is important to note that many schools are unfamiliar with selective mutism and may not understand the etiology and implications. Parents, teachers, and administrators are encouraged to learn more about selective mutism during this process, either through reading books and research articles on selective mutism or inviting a psychologist with experience in selective mutism to present information and train staff. Without proper knowledge, school interventions may not be fully effective and special education goals may be not be appropriate.

Once the child has been made eligible for an IEP or Section 504 Plan (or just an unofficial intervention plan), accommodations and interventions need to be spelled out clearly. A list of possible interventions and accommodations can be seen on page 131. From this list, it is important to highlight:

- **Of all interventions and accommodations, the most important one is desensitization in the school setting.** While the other accommodations will likely make a child much more comfortable (which is very important), the structured desensitization through stimulus fading or communication ladders is the mode through which communication begins and is generalized to the school as a whole. Intervention plans for children with SM are always a balance of providing intervention to assist in increasing communication as well as accommodations to increase comfort, social interactions with peers, and self-confidence.
- **The desensitization intervention must occur frequently and consistently; at least three times per week for fifteen minutes.** The benefits and implications of more

intensive intervention were described in chapter 5, which would suggest the benefit of even more frequent and longer practices.

- **Interventions generally start with pull-outs (i.e., the child is pulled out of the classroom to meet one-on-one with the keyworker) and progress to the keyworker "pushing in" to the classroom (i.e., the keyworker comes to the classroom and assists in generalizing attained speech to peers, teacher, and classroom activities).** The end goal for intervention is not focused on the child speaking to the keyworker—the goal is to help generalize the brave talking to the classroom and general school setting.

- **The start of the school year is a very important time for children with selective mutism, as it sets the stage for the rapport the child will have with their teacher and peers, and sets the expectation of the child as to whether they will be able to communicate this year.** It is strongly recommended that the child meet with the teacher prior to the start of the school year. The typical open house is not a good opportunity to meet and build rapport and comfort with a new teacher, as it tends to be chaotic, busy, and filled with numerous peers and parents. Instead, it is recommended that the teacher and child meet one-on-one (or with the parent). It is beneficial if this occurs both outside of the school setting (perhaps in a comfortable setting such as the child's home, the playground, the zoo, or a dog park) as well as inside the classroom setting (the child can come in a few days prior to the start of school and be a "helper" in setting up the classroom). The best generalization of speech happens when the practice occurs "in situ," or in the actual environment and situation. Thus, even after school starts, it is recommended that the child spend some time with the parent before or after school just being verbal in the school setting. This time helps the child with SM pair the academic setting with comfortable conversation. If the child is particularly anxious, even speaking to parents near the school setting can be good practice. Finally, pictures of the classroom and teacher can be used to make a "school book" to be looked at in the home, in order to prepare the child for change and get them comfortable with the new setting and teacher.

- **One possible strategy that requires very little effort by either parents or the teacher prior to school's starting is a phone call with the new teacher.** First, a few (3-5) scripted (pre-determined) questions are developed by parents that hit on the child's interests or unique experiences/characteristics (e.g., "What kind of pet do you have?" "Where did you go on your favorite vacation?"). Make sure that these questions are not yes/no (as this may inhibit speech) but require only a short response. The child first is recorded by the parent answering the questions. Then, the teacher phones the child and asks the pre-determined questions. While looking at a photo of the teacher (if possible), the child plays the recorded responses to each of the questions. In the same phone call, the questions are asked again and the child answers by speaking along with the recording. Finally, the child answers the same questions again without the recording. When the child meets the teacher in person a few days or weeks later, the questions provide a good ice-breaker for the pair and can lead to additional conversations.

Terminating Interventions

Thankfully, with effective treatment most children come to a point where they are indistinguishable from their peers in the classroom and no longer need intensive intervention. This can be determined through a classroom observation, teacher and parent interview, updated scores on the Selective Mutism Questionnaire, and qualitative knowledge of the child's abilities. It is important when determining if a child is ready to stop direct services to consider their ability both to respond *and* initiate. It is easy when a child is consistently responding to believe they do not need services, but the child still needs to be able to ask questions, advocate for themselves, and initiate verbally and nonverbally to others. When the child and teacher are fully capable of continuing the "brave practices" alone, and the child can consistently initiate and respond to most people in most situations, the keyworker may be able to decrease the frequency of meetings with the child. Consideration could be given to terminating a special education plan, bearing in mind whether the child continues to need accommodations for oral presentations, group projects, initiating with peers and adults, etc. Schools must be careful that the plan is not terminated too early—sometimes children may still need accommodations for transitioning grades or moving to a new school (i.e., middle or high school, where expectations of verbal participation are significantly increased).

In the clinical setting, services can be decreased or terminated when treatment goals are met. Generally, treatment ends when the child has experienced a significant improvement in speech and confidence, and the parent, teacher, and school feel comfortable continuing to carry out the desensitization plan.

CHAPTER 8

PAST "JUST TALKING"—
BUILDING A CHILD'S CONFIDENCE

We have spent the past seven chapters discussing strategies to increase speech. Although increasing speech in children with selective mutism is arguably the most important behavioral goal, it is only a piece of the puzzle. It is important to see the child with selective mutism as a whole, and therefore this last chapter will address some of the other potential pieces that make up the puzzle of selective mutism.

Much of what this book has discussed thus far is based on behavioral therapy (i.e., utilizing strategies to address the specific behavioral symptoms of selective mutism). Generally, practitioners do not attempt cognitive behavioral therapy with children younger than approximately 7 years of age, since cognitive intervention necessitates that children can be aware of their internal assumptions and perceptions. This ability does not typically develop until approximately the age of 6 to 9 years (depending on the child's cognitive development). For children with selective mutism who are intelligent, perceptive, and a mid-elementary or older, utilizing some cognitive strategies within the context of treatment may be beneficial.

DECREASING NEGATIVE THOUGHTS

Cognitive interventions focus on the negative or irrational thought patterns that lead to unhelpful or maladaptive behaviors. Henry Ford was correct when he stated, "Whether you think you can or think you cannot—you are right." A child who believes that they will not do well on a test may feel helpless and not attempt to study a great deal, resulting in poor testing outcomes. That maladaptive scenario began with a negative thought about ability or potential outcomes of the test. In the same way, children with selective mutism may demonstrate negative thought patterns about speaking, socializing, or interacting verbally in the classroom or public settings. Some negative or maladaptive thoughts in children with selective mutism might include:

- "I just don't have anything to say."
- "I will not be able to say it correctly."
- "If I talk, everyone will make a big deal."
- "If I get the wrong answer, people will laugh at me."
- "I have tried to talk before, and wasn't able to get the words out then. What's different this time?"

Many of these self-statements have a kernel of truth, and therefore attempting to argue with the child may not be beneficial. Instead, it is beneficial to teach the child new self-statements, script and role-play for new events, and provide them with coping strategies in case some of their fears do come true.

First, we must identify the assumptions and perceptions that accompany the fear of speaking. If the child is unable to take this step, then cognitive interventions are not recommended. In order to identify the negative assumptions, adults could ask the child questions such as, "What makes it hard to talk?" or, "What are you thinking or saying to yourself when it is hard to talk?" Many times, children describe their experience to their parents, and therefore parents can be excellent reporters on what sorts of thoughts get in the way of speaking.

If the child notes a fear of speaking incorrectly or giving an incorrect response, adults can modify their questions to reduce the fear of an incorrect answer. For example, teachers may ask the child questions in a forced-choice format, with only one obvious answer (the other choice being silly or obviously incorrect). Alternatively, the teachers may help the child practice responding in the classroom via shaping:

- First, the child practices raising their hand to show knowledge, with the understanding that the teacher will not call on them.
- Second, the teacher lets the child know that they will be calling on them during a specific time of the lesson, and tells the child exactly what they will be asking so that the child knows the answer with certainty.
- Third, the teacher calls on the child without preparation, but only if the child's hand is raised. Children with SM should not be called on randomly if they are not indicating knowledge of the answer.

If the child fears that other children will overreact when they speak, the child could write a letter to peers asking them to please not "make a big deal out of it" when they do speak. It is important that peers and adults know to be matter-of-fact and calm when the child talks—pointing out that they spoke and asking them repeatedly to speak again likely increases the child's anxiety.

Cognitive restructuring, or changing maladaptive thought patterns, involves identifying negative thoughts, challenging them, and replacing them with more appropriate, balanced, helpful thoughts. For example, if a child believes that because they were not able to speak in the past they will not be able to speak in the future, the interventionist can work with the child to determine whether that sort of statement holds true. Excellent workbooks exist for cognitive intervention, including *Coping Cat* by Phillip C. Kendall and Kristina A. Hedtke (www.copingcat.net) and *Think Good, Feel Good* by Paul Stallard for younger children and *The Shyness and Social Anxiety Workbook for Teens* by Jennifer Shannon for adolescents.

INCREASING SELF-CONFIDENCE

Think of a time recently when you felt really self-confident. What were you doing? What had just occurred? For most of us, self-confidence comes both from feeling that others value you and feeling successful, worthy, or talented. Some ways to increase self-confidence in kids with selective mutism include:

- **Spend uninterrupted time with your child.** Play what they want to play. Talk about what they want to talk about. Do what they want to do, and follow their lead. Special time like this helps children feel valued, loved, and appreciated.

- **Help the child build success in speaking through the slow, steady steps outlined in this book.** Success builds on success, and even small steps are movements in the right direction.

- **Make a "Brave Chart" for your refrigerator at home (if you are a parent) or office at school (if you are a keyworker), and list the brave activities or brave work your child has accomplished.** Remind them frequently of all their accomplishments, and how much braver and stronger they have become. Encourage teens to document on their phones or journal all of the steps they have taken (even the small ones) and look back at it on a regular basis.

- **Praise success, but also praise efforts.** Life is not always about outcomes; sometimes children try very hard but are not quite successful. They should be praised for their efforts.

- **Encourage the child to develop talents that are not speech-based.** For example, many children with SM are wonderful singers, beautiful dancers, or talented soccer players. Children need to feel that they are good at something, and these extracurricular activities not only allow them to feel talented but also provide excellent social opportunities for brave practices.

- **Display self-confidence yourself.** Self-confidence is not the absence of worry or nervousness; it is the ability to stand and act in the face of those feelings. When a situation comes up that makes you feel nervous, tell the child your worries (assuming that the situation is age-appropriate and does not directly involve the child). Then, tell the child the confident self-statements that help you be brave in the face of worry. For example, if you have a big deadline at work, you might explain to the child that you feel nervous thinking that you cannot finish in time. However, you have finished projects before deadlines in the past, and you know that if you work hard you are completely capable of finishing.

SOCIAL SKILLS TRAINING

Research does not demonstrate a fundamental deficit in social skill acquisition for children with selective mutism. However, since kids with SM have significantly fewer social interactions, it is not uncommon that they are socially immature, lack some social awareness, or don't demonstrate age-appropriate social skills. Social skills training or role-playing social interactions can be helpful for two reasons.

First, it helps children "script" social situations. A script is a sequence of expected behaviors for a situation. Most adults have a script for social situations. If you are going to the doctor's office, the script likely includes checking in, sitting in the waiting room until you are called, relocating to an examination room, and speaking to the physician. Then you will check out at the front desk and leave. Without a script, anxiety and uncertainty would reign. What if you were going to go to the doctor's office, but you had no idea what would occur there? You did not know how much you were expected to pay, what the doctor would do or say, whether you would be safe or unsafe, and who might be allowed to see you in one of those open-backed gowns. In situations without scripts, most individuals feel ill-prepared, uncertain, anxious, and avoidant. Scripts help not only to reduce anxiety but also to build new language, social, and activity routines for children (Barnett et al., 2007). Possible scripts include how to order at a restaurant, interrupt someone who is not already attentive to you, introduce yourself, ask a friend to play, etc.

Second, social skills training allows the opportunity to learn and practice social interactions in a safe, comfortable setting. When teaching a new skill, adults often stop when the child seems to have initially mastered the skill, and then expect that the child will easily utilize that new skill in each and every situation. "Overlearning" is a term used for practicing much beyond the initial mastery of a newly acquired skill; overlearning leads to expanded mastery and automaticity of a skill. The Yerkes-Dodson law predicts that overlearning will significantly increase the use of the behavior even in high-arousal states (Rohrer, 2005). In layman's terms, if a child practices a social behavior to the point of complete and total mastery and even beyond to the point of boredom, it becomes automatic and therefore can be done in their sleep, with their eyes closed, and standing on their head. This is exactly what we want for children with SM when they approach the counter at McDonalds® and the clerk asks them what they would like, their response and the back-and-forth banter of ordering should be so ingrained and over-practiced that, despite their increasing level of anxiety (and therefore emotional arousal), they are simply programmed to respond without even thinking. This type of over-practice takes . . . a lot of practice. Role playing should be part of the child's normal day. Children should be role-playing with parents, keyworkers, therapists, and others in preparation for social interactions. A good rule of thumb is that the more realistic the scenario, the more effective the role-play. For example, if the role-lay is in preparation for an upcoming presentation, it is wonderful to practice that presentation at home, in the car, and at a friend's house. However, the most effective role-play might be in the classroom where the presentation will be given, at the microphone, and with the prompts that will be used in the actual presentation. Likewise, if a child is role-playing to ask a peer over for a play date, a role-play done on the playground (where they are planning to ask) and with another peer whom they already feel comfortable with is likely to be most effective.

Social stories also offer social skills training through a medium most children find entertaining—books, videos, and phone apps. A social story is a visual or written guide to a variety of social interactions, situations, or skills for which the child may need preparation. The goal of social stories is to provide accurate and understandable steps in a social situation, allowing the child to see the likely stages and outcomes of an experience prior to experiencing it themselves. There are many sites providing general social stories, such as Sandbox Learning (http://www.sandbox-learning.com/) or the Social Story® Creator and Library® app by Touch Autism. It is also easy and fun to create your own social stories by making a book with your child relating how a social interaction will take place.

PREDICTABILITY AND CONTROL

Humans feel anxiety because of a lack of predictability and a feeling of a lack of control. If something is under your control and you know exactly what will happen, you are not worried or stressed about it. We only worry when we do not feel in control or do not know what will happen next.

Children with selective mutism also desire predictability and control. Certain things cannot be completely controlled, such as the social responses children might receive from peers when they speak (although we can try to remind peers of the appropriate response when speech occurs). However, the more control and predictability we can provide to a child with selective mutism, the more the child will feel a reduction in anxiety and a feeling of mastery. For example:

Be consistent. I cannot highlight enough the importance of being consistent with anxious children. Consistency takes many forms:

- **Be consistent and predictable in your intervention.** Kids should understand the next steps, the overall goal of getting braver, and the strategies that will be used. My sessions always run in the exact same manner—I am very predictable. The activity might be different, and the goal changes from session to session, but the child knows how long the meeting will last, what sorts of steps we will be working on, and that I will never move too quickly for them.

- **Be consistent with your discipline and expectations.** I strongly believe that children with selective mutism should not be given a "pass" on unacceptable behavior. Many teachers tell me that they allow the child with SM to get away with not following the rules of the classroom because they don't want to upset him or her. For example, a teacher recently told me that a patient of mine had been blatantly copying off of another student in the classroom, right under the eyes of the teacher. She knew it was going on, and had reminded the class as a whole of the rules, but he had not stopped and she had done nothing about it because she was afraid of his reaction. Of course we must first make sure that there is nothing else prohibiting the child from doing his own work (i.e., Does he have a learning disorder and not understand? Was there a lack of understanding of the directions, but he could not ask for clarification so he was leaning over to determine what he should be doing?). We considered all of these possibilities and came to the conclusion that he was simply cheating. I gave permission to the teacher to tell him in no uncertain terms that cheating would no longer be accepted, and he immediately stopped. Children with SM must be held to the same behavioral expectations as peers, assuming that the behavior is not speech-related.

- **Be consistent in the classroom.** Children with SM tend to enjoy visual schedules. If there is going to be a significant change in the day, let them know the change and how that will impact them. If possible, keep their school day consistent and predictable.

- **Be consistent at home.** Kids need a predictable daily schedule, predictable bedtimes, predictable routines, and predictable responses from parents. Children with anxiety thrive on predictability and consistency in the home. I know how difficult it can be to stay predictable—life throws curveballs in terms of scheduling, parents are tired and are not always consistent with discipline approaches, and activities sometimes allow kids to stay up much later than they should. I understand that life can be chaotic, but be *as predictable as possible.*

- **Give the child some control over their intervention.** We learn as parents that kids need to have a sense of control in their daily lives, such as picking out their own clothing and deciding what they want to drink with dinner. We quickly learn to give them choices that we as adults are equally comfortable with; in that way, both the child and adult can be happy with the outcome. The same strategy can be used in behavioral intervention. For example, when I move to the step of blowing air, I often give children several choices of how we can practice blowing air (i.e., "We are going to practice blowing air, and we could use a balloon, a pinwheel, or a candle—which would you like to use to practice?"). I am equally comfortable with all of those options, but I am giving the child the ability to decide what type of practice we will do. At the step of making sounds, I may put letters of the alphabet on cards and allow the child to choose which sounds to start with. Eventually we will do all of the sounds, but it gives the child a sense of control over the progression. When it is time to speak to someone new or use their voice in a new setting, I give many choices of people or places and allow the child to pick. I do not ask the child if they would like to blow air, or if they would like to talk to someone new, because I can almost guarantee what the answer will be. Instead, I give several acceptable options.

THE ART OF RELAXING

Relaxation training is a common behavioral intervention for anxiety, and training children with selective mutism how to relax their bodies and minds is valuable. Typically, teaching relaxation training at the start of the intervention proves to be difficult, since relaxation training generally includes deep breathing (which may be anxiety-provoking when children are beginning treatment with a novel adult). Thus, I either train parents on how to teach their child to relax at home or I wait until the child begins to feel comfortable with me in the clinic before I begin relaxation training.

Common characteristics of children with SM include, 1) becoming easily aroused in social or public situations; 2) stiff, awkward body postures due to anxiety; and, 3) difficulty returning to baseline. Progressive muscle relaxation, along with mindfulness training (i.e., training in the awareness of thoughts, feelings, and physiological responses) and diaphragmatic breathing helps teach body awareness and awareness of breathing and the senses. Often, children with SM are extremely guarded with their body movements and are too embarrassed to participate in relaxation strategies with a therapist. Working first on mindfulness, including mindful listening, mindful observing, and mindful touching can be less anxiety-provoking and therefore a good place to start. *The MindUP Curriculum* by the Hawn Foundation outlines activities that can be used to teach mindfulness to any age group.

When a child becomes more comfortable in the clinic, progressive muscle relaxation and diaphragmatic breathing can be taught through a variety of methods. Scripts are available for progressive muscle relaxation; these scripts walk children verbally through the tensing and relaxing of their major muscle groups. *I Can Relax!* by Donna Pincus and *Still Quiet Place: Mindfulness for Young Children* by Amy Salzman provides sound effects and music with a narrator who leads the child through muscle relaxation and visualization.

An example of a progressive muscle relaxation script might include (Adapted from Koeppen, 1974):

PROGRESSIVE MUSCLE RELAXATION SCRIPT

"Today we're going to practice some special kinds of exercises called relaxation exercises. These exercises help you to learn how to relax when you're feeling uptight and help you get rid of those butterflies-in-your-stomach kinds of feelings. They're also kind of neat because you can learn how to do some of them without anyone really noticing.

In order for you to get the best feelings from these exercises, there are some rules you must follow. First, you need to do exactly what I say, even if it seems kind of silly. Second, you must try hard to do what I say. Third, you must pay attention to your body. Throughout these exercises, pay attention to how your muscles feel when they are tight and when they are loose and relaxed. And fourth, you must practice. The more you practice, the more relaxed you can get. Do you have any questions?

Are you ready to begin? Okay, first, get as comfortable as you can in your chair. Sit back, get both feet on the floor, and just let your arms hang loose. That's fine. Now close your eyes and try to keep them closed as we practice. Remember to follow my instructions very carefully, try hard, and pay attention to your body. Here we go."

Pretend you have a whole lemon in your left hand. *Now squeeze it hard. Try to squeeze all the juice out. Feel the tightness in your hand and arm as you squeeze. Now drop the lemon. Notice how your muscles feel when they are relaxed. Take another lemon and squeeze. Try to squeeze this one harder than you did the first one. That's right. Real hard. Now drop the lemon and relax. See how much better your hand and arm feel when they are relaxed. Once again, take a lemon in your left hand and squeeze all the juice out. Don't leave a single drop. Squeeze hard. Good. Now relax and let the lemon fall from your hand. (Repeat the process for the right hand and arm.)*

Pretend you are a furry, lazy cat. *You want to stretch. Stretch your arms out in front of you. Raise them up high over your head. Way back. Feel the pull in your shoulders. Stretch higher. Now just let your arms drop back to your side. Okay, let's stretch again. Stretch your arms out in front of you. Raise them over your head. Pull them back, way back. Pull hard. Now let them drop quickly. Good. Notice how your shoulders feel more relaxed. This time let's have a great big stretch. Try to touch the ceiling. Stretch your arms way out in front of you. Raise them way up high over your head. Push them way, way back. Notice the tension and pull in your arms and shoulders. Hold tight, now. Great. Let them drop very quickly and feel how good it is to be relaxed. It feels good and warm and lazy.*

Now pretend you have a giant jawbreaker bubble gum in your mouth. *It's very hard to chew. Bite down on it. Hard. Let your neck muscles help you. Now relax. Just let your jaw hang loose. Notice that how good it feels just to let your jaw drop. Okay, let's tackle that jawbreaker again now. Bite down. Hard. Try to squeeze it out between your teeth. That's good. You're really tearing that gum up. Now relax again. It feels good just to let go and not have to fight that bubble gum. Okay, one more time. Bite down. Hard as you can. Oh, you're really working hard. Good. Now relax. Try to relax your whole body. Let yourself go as loose as you can.*

Here comes a pesky old fly. *He has landed on your nose. Try to get him off without using your hands. That's right, wrinkle up your nose. Make as many wrinkles in your nose as you can. Scrunch your nose up real hard. Good. You've chased him away. Now you can relax your nose. Oops, here he comes back again. Right back in the middle of your nose. Wrinkle up your nose again. Shoo him off. Wrinkle it up hard. Hold it just as tight as you can. Okay, he flew away. You can relax your face. Notice that when you scrunch up your nose, your cheeks and your mouth and your forehead and your eyes all help you, and they get tight too. So when you relax your nose, your whole body relaxes too, and that feels good. Oh-oh. This time that old fly has come back, but this time he's on your forehead. Make lots of wrinkles. Try to catch him between all those wrinkles. Hold it tight, now. Okay, you can let go. He's gone for good. Now you can just relax. Let your face go smooth, no wrinkles anywhere. Your face feels nice and smooth and relaxed.*

Hey. *Here comes a cute baby elephant. But he's not watching where he's going. He doesn't see you lying in the grass, and he's about to step on your stomach. Don't move. You don't have time to get out of the way. Just get ready for him. Make your stomach very hard. Tighten up your stomach muscles real tight. Hold it. It looks like he is going the other way. You can relax now. Let your stomach go soft. Let it be as relaxed as you can. That feels so much better. Oops, he's coming this way again. Get Ready. Tighten up your stomach. Make your stomach into a rock. Okay, he's moving away again. You can relax now. Kind of settle down, get comfortable, and relax. Notice the difference between a tight stomach and a relaxed one. That's how we want to feel—nice and loose and relaxed. You won't believe this, but this time he's coming your way and no turning around. He's headed straight for you. Tighten up. Here he comes. This is really it. You've got to hold on tight. He's stepping on you. He's stepped over you. Now he's gone for good. You can relax completely. You're safe. Everything is okay, and you can feel nice and relaxed.*

This time imagine that you want to squeeze through a narrow fence and the boards have splinters on them. *You'll have to make yourself very skinny if you're going to make it through. Suck your stomach in. Try to squeeze it up against your backbone. Try to be skinny as you can. You've got to be skinny now. Just relax and feel your stomach being warm and loose. Okay, let's try to get through that fence now. Squeeze up your stomach. Make it touch your backbone. Get it real small and tight. Get it as skinny as you can. Hold tight, now. You've got to squeeze through. You got through that narrow little fence and no splinters. You can relax now. Settle back and let your stomach come back out where it belongs. You can feel really good now. You've done fine.*

Now pretend that you are standing barefoot in a big, fat mud puddle. *Squish your toes down deep into the mud. Try to get your feet down to the bottom of the mud puddle. You'll probably need your legs to help you push. Push down, spread your toes apart, feel the mud squish up between your toes. Now step out of the mud puddle. Relax your feet. Let your toes go loose and feel how nice that it feels to be relaxed. Back into the* *mud puddle. Squish your toes down. Let your leg muscles help push your feet down. Push your feet. Hard. Try to squeeze that puddle dry. Okay. Come back out now. Relax your feet, relax your legs, relax your toes. It feels so good to be relaxed. No tenseness anywhere. You feel kind of warm and tingly.*

Stay as relaxed as you can. *Let your whole body go limp and feel all your muscles relaxed. In a few minutes I will ask you to open your eyes, and that will be the end of this practice session. As you go through the day, remember how good it feels to be relaxed. Sometimes you have to make yourself tighter before you can be relaxed, just as we did in these exercises. Practice these exercises everyday to get more and more relaxed. A good time to practice is at night, after you have gone to bed and the lights are out and you won't be disturbed. It will help you get to sleep. Then, when you are really a good relaxer, you can help yourself relax at school. Just remember the elephant, or the jaw breaker, or the mud puddle, and you can do our exercises and nobody will know. Today is a good day, and you are ready to feel very relaxed. You've worked hard and it feels good to work hard. Very slowly, now, open your eyes and wiggle your muscles around a little. Very good. You've done a good job. You're going to be a super relaxer.*

Apps are also available for bodily self-awareness and relaxation, including Cardiograph (an app measuring heart rate through the iPhone) and BellyBio® (interactive breathing through biofeedback). Children tend to find these apps fun and engaging, and it keeps them interested in the relaxation process. Biodots® (www.biodots.net) are also enjoyable additions to relaxation training. Biodots are small stickers which gauge skin temperature (a common measurement of physiological stress and anxiety) and change colors accordingly.

After teaching children how to relax, they are sent home with the project of practicing relaxation, since skills cannot be used in the midst of stress unless they are practiced frequently. Parents and children log their heart rate and Biodot® color before and after relaxation in order to observe change through relaxation.

Relaxation Log

Date Practiced	Heart Rate Before?	Color Before?	Heart Rate After?	Color After?

CONCLUSION

Physicians, psychologists, teachers, and others constantly sing the praises of early intervention for a multitude of developmental and psychological disorders in childhood. Early intervention of special needs can improve outcomes, lessen the effects of the condition, and teach others to support the child and family in a successful manner. Too frequently children with selective mutism do not receive early intervention. The most common reasons include:

- A lag in time between observation of an issue (i.e., the difficulty speaking in public) and diagnosis/intervention. If you are reading this book, you are better prepared to help curb this delay (congratulations). Please consider helping others find out about selective mutism by educating your school staff, pediatrician, family, and friends. Send out informational brochures. Talk to others about your experience. Spread awareness.

- Difficulty finding specialists who can help. This is a particularly difficult issue, because many psychologists still do not know enough about selective mutism. Look specifically for a psychologist with experience treating kids with anxiety using behavioral therapy, or visit www.selectivemutism.org, www.adaa.org, or www.abct.org to find appropriate referrals.

- Concerns about "labeling" the child. Trust me, the child knows that they do not talk. This is no secret and it is not a valid reason for continuing without intervention.

- Family members who are not supportive. Everyone has one—a family member who believes the child is "just fine" or thinks that all they need is more discipline in the home. One of the hardest parts about being a parent is making unpopular decisions with the knowledge that it will improve the child's life in the long-run.

- Belief that the child will grow out of it. There are children with SM who improve significantly with time and maturity. And there are children who do not improve with time, and instead experience an increase in anxiety, a reduction in friends, and difficulty being successful in school. We do not know which group a given child will fall into—should we really roll the dice?

Research demonstrates that the most important predictors of treatment success are the age of the child upon treatment, the duration of symptoms, and whether the children obtains behavioral intervention (Pionek Stone, 2002). We must intervene as soon as possible and effectively to produce the best outcomes in children and adolescents with selective mutism. The time is now.

TREATMENT FORMS
AND HANDOUTS

DIAGNOSTIC INTERVIEW

Name: _____   Date of Intake: _____

Date of Birth: _____   Age: _____

Informants: _____

School: _____

Special Education Certification:

☐ Speech/Language Impaired (SLI) or Communication Impaired (CI)

☐ Other Health Impaired (OHI)

☐ Emotionally Impaired/Disabled (EI/ED)

☐ Specific Learning Disability (SLD)

☐ Autistic Impairment (AI)

☐ Other Designation: _____

☐ Section 504 Plan

☐ None and parents are not interested in pursuing

☐ None but parents interested in pursuing

Current Services

☐ Physical Therapy

☐ Occupational Therapy

☐ Social Work

☐ Speech

☐ Resource Room

☐ Other: _____

Evaluation/Treatment History:

Previous Evaluations: _____

_____
_____
_____
_____
_____
_____
_____
_____
_____
_____

Previous Treatment: _____

_____

_____

_____

_____

_____

_____

_____

_____

_____

_____

_____

_____

_____

Tutoring: _____

_____

_____

_____

_____

_____

_____

_____

_____

_____

_____

_____

_____

Medications (past/present): _____

_____

_____

_____

_____

_____

_____

_____

_____

_____

_____

_____

_____

_____

Presenting Concerns: _____

_____

_____

_____

_____

_____

_____

_____

_____

_____

_____

_____

_____

_____

_____

Educational History/Concerns: _____

_____

_____

_____

_____

_____

_____

_____

_____

_____

_____

_____

_____

_____

_____

Strengths: _____

_____

_____

_____

_____

_____

_____

_____

_____

_____

_____

_____

_____

_____

Speaking Situations Assessment

At School (i.e., teacher, specials teachers, female peers, male peers, principal, other adults in the school)

How? (what type of communication—nonverbal, whispered, regular speech, etc.)	Where? (what location)	Who? (whom do they talk to)

In Public (i.e., waiters, clerks, librarians, extracurricular teachers/coaches)

How? (what type of communication—nonverbal, whispered, regular speech, etc.)	Where? (what location)	Who? (whom do they talk to)

To Extended Family and Family Friends (i.e., grandparents, aunts/uncles, cousins, friends, friend's parents)

How? (what type of communication—nonverbal, whispered, regular speech, etc.)	Where? (what location)	Who? (whom do they talk to)

Medical History:

Prenatal/Neonatal:

Labor/Delivery:

Infancy/Early Childhood:

Recurrent Medical Problems:

Medications Used Chronically:

Hospitalizations/Surgeries:

Seizures/Head Injuries:

Review of Systems:

	Parent Concern	Not a Parent Concern	Notes. . .
Sleep Issues			
Feeding/Appetite			
Hearing			
Vision			
Allergies			
Bedwetting			
Daytime Accidents			
Repetitive/Restrictive Interests			
Eye Contact			
Worries/Anxieties			
Strange Rituals or Odd Habits			
Odd Sounds			
School Refusal/Anxiety			
Separation Anxiety			
Sensory Issues			
Regular Stomach aches, Headaches, or Muscle Tension			
Behavioral Issues at Home			
Behavioral Issues at School			

Developmental History:

Fine and Gross Motor:

Language:

What is the primary language?

Are other languages spoken at home?

Articulation, Fluency, or Speech Difficulties:

Social Skills:

Environment:

Family Members:

Name	Relation to Child	Age	Occupation	Notes. . .

Parent's Relationship: _____

Family Mental Health History:

Stressors (i.e., Educational, health, financial, neighborhood, or family issues)

Therapy:

What changes do you hope intervention will lead to?

What are you afraid will happen if presenting concerns are not addressed?

How long do you think these changes will take?

STAGES OF SOCIAL COMMUNICATION COMFORT SCALE

NON-COMMUNICATIVE—neither non-verbal nor verbal. **NO social engagement.**

STAGE 0—NO RESPONDING, NO INITIATING

– Child stands motionless (stiff body language), expressionless, averts eye gaze, appears "frozen," **MUTE**

OR

– Seemingly IGNORES person while interacting or speaking to other(s). **MUTE towards others**

For communication to occur, Social Engagement must occur

COMMUNICATIVE (Nonverbal and/or Verbal)*

*To advance from one stage of communication to the next, increasing social comfort needs to occur.

STAGE 1—NONVERBAL COMMUNICATION: (NV)

1A Responding—pointing, nodding, writing, sign language, gesturing, use of "objects" (e.g., whistles, bells, Non-voice augmentative device (e.g., communication boards/cards, symbols, photos)

1B Initiating—getting someone's attention via pointing, gesturing, writing, use of "objects" to get attention (e.g., whistles, bells, Non-voice augmentative device (e.g., communication boards/cards, symbols, photos)

STAGE 2—TRANSITION INTO VERBAL COMMUNICATION (TV)

2A Responding—Via any sounds, (e.g., grunts, animal sounds, letter sounds, moans, etc.): Verbal Intermediary® or Whisper Buddy; Augmentative Device with sound, (e.g., simple message switch, multiple voice message device, tape recorder, video, etc.)

2B Initiating—Getting someone's attention via any sounds, (e.g., grunts, animal sounds, letter sounds, moans, etc.): Verbal Intermediary® or Whisper Buddy; Augmentative Device with sound, (e.g., simple message switch, multiple voice message device, tape recorder, video, etc)

STAGE 3—VERBAL COMMUNICATION (VC)

3A Responding—Approximate speech/direct speech (e.g., altered or made-up language, baby talk, reading/rehearsing script, soft whispering, speaking)

3B Initiating—Approximate speech/direct speech (e.g., altered or made-up language, baby talk, reading/rehearsing script, soft whispering, speaking)

STRUCTURED OBSERVATION SHEET

Directions: For each column, circle/check all that apply.

Condition	Whom did child communicate to?	What did child say?	How did child communicate?	Strategies utilized:	Effective?
Alone with parent	Parent Sibling	Respond Initiate	Nonverbal Whisper Altered Voice One Word 2-3 words Longer utterance	Verbal praise Verbal prompt Gesture prompt Allow for delayed response	Y/N Y/N Y/N Y/N

Comments:

_____

_____

_____

| Novel person enters but no attention to child | Parent

Sibling

Novel person | Respond

Initiate | Nonverbal
Whisper
Altered Voice/
Appearance
One word
2-3 words
Longer utterance | Verbal praise
Verbal prompt
Gesture
Prompt
Allow for delayed response | Y/N
Y/N
Y/N
Y/N |

Comments:

_____

_____

_____

| Novel person attends and reflects but no questions | Parent

Sibling

Novel person | Respond

Initiate | Nonverbal
Whisper
Altered Voice/
Appearance
One word
2-3 words
Longer utterance | Verbal praise
Verbal prompt
Gesture
Prompt
Allow for delayed response | Y/N
Y/N
Y/N
Y/N |

Comments:

_____

_____

_____

Directions: For each column, circle/check all that apply.

| Nonverbal demands from novel person (pointing, holding up fingers, yes/no questions) | Parent

Sibling

Novel person | Respond

Initiate | Nonverbal
Whisper
Altered Voice/
Appearance
One word
2-3 words
Longer utterance | Verbal praise
Verbal prompt
Gesture
Prompt
Allow for delayed response | Y/N
Y/N
Y/N
Y/N |

Comments:

_____

_____

_____

| Verbal demands from novel person
1. Yes/no question
2. Forced choice question
3. Open-ended question | Parent

Sibling

Novel person | Respond

Initiate | Nonverbal
Whisper
Altered Voice/
Appearance
One Word
2-3 words
Longer utterance | Verbal praise
Verbal prompt
Gesture
prompt
Allow for delayed response | Y/N
Y/N
Y/N
Y/N |

Comments:

_____

_____

_____

| Alone with family again | Parent

Sibling | Respond

Initiate | Nonverbal
Whisper
Altered Voice/
Appearance
One Word
2-3 words
Longer utterance | Verbal praise
Verbal prompt
Gesture
prompt
Allow for delayed response | Y/N
Y/N
Y/N
Y/N |

Comments:

_____

_____

_____

FUNCTIONAL BEHAVIORAL ANALYSIS

Structured Functional Behavior Analysis Selective Mutism—SCHOOL

Child: _____ Date: _____ Time of Assessment: _____

Behavior:																						
Response*																						
Nonverbal Response																						
Lack of Response																						
Location:																						
Regular Classroom																						
Specials Classroom																						
Outside/Recess																						
Library																						
Lunchroom																						
Immediate Antecedent:																						
Peer-initiated Interaction																						
Adult-initiated Interaction																						
Interaction initiated to group																						
Child has need																						
Child is socially motivated																						
Immediate Consequence:																						
Redirected to enjoyable activity																						
Saved***																						
Lack of Response Time																						

(Continued)

Immediate Consequence:

No Response/Ignored												
Punitive Statement												
Interrupted												
Prompted to verbalize												
Response/Reciprocation***												

Indicate:
* Voiced or **W**hispered
** **1:1**, **S**mall Group (</= 5) or Large Group (>6)
*** **P**eer or **A**dult

Prompt	R+	Escape	Strat.	Pun.
Total:				

STIMULUS FADING PROCEDURE (EXAMPLE)

1. Goal is to get new communication partner (NCP) into room with child using appropriate speech. Parent or keyworker's job is to keep child talking while the NCP enters through fun activities that encourage speech, forced-choice questions, and at least five-second latency to response.

2. Parent/keyworker and child should have some time to "warm up" in the room, playing and talking alone with the door almost closed. During this time, full speech (not a quiet whisper) must be obtained consistently before a new individual begins fading in. (***If several sessions pass and the child cannot warm up to the point of consistent speech, intervention must shift to shaping).

3. NCP begins fading into the room when the parent/keyworker has obtained an appropriate volume of consistent speech from the child. The NCP begins by simply opening the door and walking in front of the door, so as to make her presence known. The NCP should NOT respond in any way to what the child says or act as if they are attending to the child.

4. The NCP should very slowly enter the room, as far away from the child as possible, and busy themselves (i.e., type on the computer, pick up the room, or do paperwork). If the child begins to discontinue speaking or shows other general signs of anxiety, slow the entrance down even more or just stay in the same position for several minutes until the anxiety is reduced and speech resumes.

5. The NCP should slowly start making their way toward the child by finding things to do in closer proximity to the interaction, but should continue to pay no attention to the child.

6. When the NCP is close to the interaction and the child has maintained speech, he or she can begin to silently attend to the interaction.

7. If the child tolerates attention to their speech, the NCP can begin to reflect or respond to what the child is saying. For example, if the child tells the parent that they picked a blue card, the NCP could reflect, "Oh, you picked a blue card." If the child tells the mother that he played his new videogame last night, the NCP could comment, "You played your new game—that sounds like fun."

8. When this seems comfortable and minimally anxiety-provoking, the NCP can begin peppering in occasional forced-choice questions.

9. When the child is consistently responding to the NCP, the parent can begin to slowly fade out of the room, leaving the NCP and the child. This can be done using the above steps in reverse. It is important that the parent not fade faster than the child can manage. If significant anxiety is observed or if the child's verbalizations considerably decrease, the parent should remain at the current location until comfort is re-established.

If the child ceases speech at any point during the stimulus fading, the NCP should stop moving toward the child/parent and wait for the parent to re-establish speech with the child.

In the case that the parent is unable to re-establish speech in a few minutes, the NCP should move back a few steps toward the door, and again see if the parent is able to re-establish speech with the child. If the parents is still unable to re-establish speech, shaping may need to be considered in the place of stimulus fading as the initial intervention.

If the NCP is unable to complete all steps in one session, they could start outside of the room again but attempt to fade in more quickly. As the child's anxiety will likely spontaneously return somewhat at the beginning of each session (although less and less will be present each time), the NCP should still be careful to be responsive to the anxiety.

COMMUNICATION LADDER HANDOUT

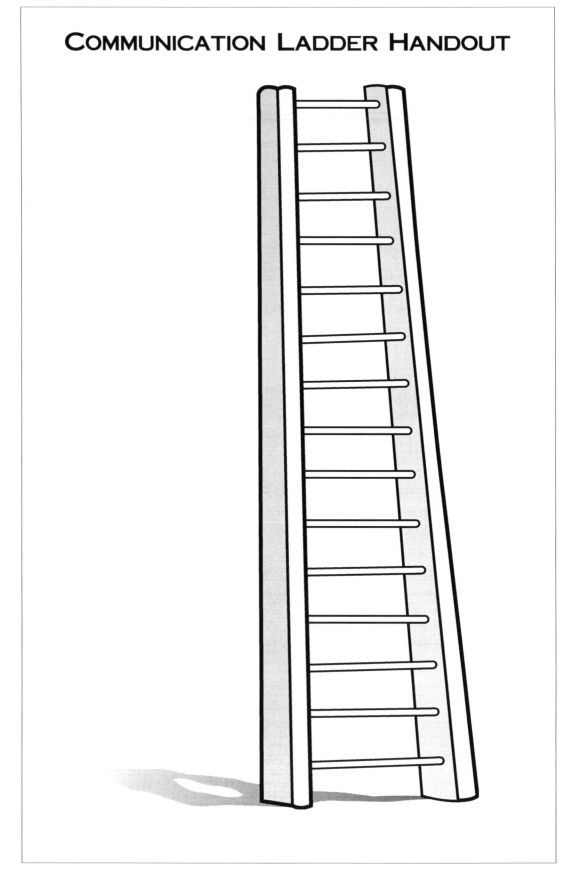

PLAYDATE DATA SHEET

Classmate's Name	Description of Speech Prior to Play date (e.g., nonverbal, sounds, one word answers, etc.)	Description of Speech During/After Play date	Spoken to Classmate's Parent(s)?	Number of Past Play dates With This Friend?	Other Comments:
Joe Smith	Ben had never spoken to Joe prior to the play date.	Ben initiated by asking Joe questions during their play date.	No.	2	This was Ben's first play date with speech in a full voice.

PERSON BINGO

Have you ever been to Disneyworld?	Do you own a dog?	Can you speak another language?
Are you the oldest child in your family?	Do you like Mexican food?	Do you like funny movies?
Were you born in March?	Have you lived in more than one house?	Have you ever owned a fish?

FAVORITES GAME

Favorite	Name: _____	Name: _____	Name: _____
Movie			
Ice Cream Flavor			
Book			
Pizza Topping			

EXAMPLE MISSION CARDS

Ask the nurse for a paperclip.	Tell someone in your class that you like their outfit.
Find out what your teacher did this weekend.	Ask the teacher to borrow a pencil.
Take this letter to the principal and ask him to mail it.	Ask the secretary if there is any mail for your teacher today.
Say "Hi" to your music teacher.	Ask your teacher if you can use the bathroom.

SCRIPTED INITIATION SHEET

Task	Date Completed							
Good morning teacher.								
goodbye.								
May I have _____ please?								
I need help with . . .								
May I please go to the bathroom?								
May I get a drink of water?								
Thank you.								

****Children tend to need 7-10 practices of each scripted statement before it becomes comfortable/ less anxiety-provoking. Following each successful practice, they are rewarded with a sticker; after filling up the page they have earned a large prize. Two boxes are left blank to personalize to the child's specific practice needs.

BRAVE WORK LOG (EXAMPLE)

Date	Environment	Communication Partner	Step on Ladder (mark all that apply)	Notes
3/13/14	Social Worker's office	Ms. Brandez (keyworker)	☐ Nonverbals ☐ Sounds ☐ Whispers ☒ One word Response ☐ Multiple Word Response ☐ Initiation ☐ Regular Volume of Voice	Jack did a great job. He spoke directly to both Ms. Brandez and Mr. Jones.
		Mr. Jones (English teacher)		

Date	Environment	Communication Partner	Step on Ladder	Notes
3/15/14	Grandma's house	Mom	☐ Nonverbals ☐ Sounds ☐ Whispers ☐ One word Response ☐ Multiple Word Response ☒ Initiation ☐ Regular Volume of Voice	Wow, Jack has come so far. Now he talks to Grandma as soon as she comes to the house!
		Grandma Jackson		

Date	Environment	Communication Partner	Step on Ladder	Notes
3/16/14	McDonalds	clerk	☐ Nonverbals ☐ Sounds ☒ Whispers ☐ One word Response ☐ Multiple Word Response ☐ Initiation ☐ Regular Volume of Voice	Jack was hesitant to order, but was able to order in a whisper while looking at mom (but at a loud enough volume that the clerk could hear).
		Mom		

Date	Environment	Communication Partner	Step on Ladder	Notes
			☐ Nonverbals ☐ Sounds ☐ Whispers ☐ One word Response ☐ Multiple Word Response	

Date	Environment	Communication Partner	Step on Ladder (mark all that apply)	Notes
			☐ Nonverbals ☐ Sounds ☐ Whispers ☒ One word Response ☐ Multiple Word Response ☐ Initiation ☐ Regular Volume of Voice	

Date	Environment	Communication Partner	Step on Ladder	Notes
			☐ Nonverbals ☐ Sounds ☐ Whispers ☐ One word Response ☐ Multiple Word Response ☒ Initiation ☐ Regular Volume of Voice	

Date	Environment	Communication Partner	Step on Ladder	Notes
			☐ Nonverbals ☐ Sounds ☒ Whispers ☐ One word Response ☐ Multiple Word Response ☒ Initiation ☐ Regular Volume of Voice	

Date	Environment	Communication Partner	Step on Ladder	Notes
			☐ Nonverbals ☐ Sounds ☐ Whispers ☐ One word Response ☐ Multiple Word Response ☐ Initiation ☐ Regular Volume of Voice	

UNDERSTANDING SELECTIVE MUTISM HANDOUT

Selective mutism is a childhood anxiety disorder characterized by a child's 'inability' to speak in various social settings. These children are able to speak freely at home, and in settings where they are comfortable, secure and relaxed.

Selective mutism is due to severe anxiety, not oppositional behavior directed towards school personnel—the lack of communication serves to reduce anxiety and protect the child from further anxiety-provoking social interactions. It is so important for teachers, school personnel, and other adults to remember that the child with selective mutism is not 'being silent' or barely whispering 'on purpose,' or trying to 'control' a situation. These children literally **cannot** speak.

The majority of selectively mute children have **inhibited temperaments.** When children who are selectively mute confront a social situation where they do not feel comfortable, they often become mute and possibly non-communicative. Some children may have great difficulty pointing/nodding or even mouthing words while others may be able to respond and initiate nonverbally with ease and 'look' completely relaxed.

School is usually the most difficult place for children with selective mutism to be. What can an adult do to help the anxious child with selective mutism?

- Primarily, the adult should try to get to know the child in a completely unobtrusive and accepting manner. Visiting the child at home is often beneficial. There is certainly no better place for children to feel more comfortable then in their own home! Visiting the children on their own turf will certainly allow for a more comfortable way of getting to know each other.

- Be patient with the child. Although he/she may seem stubborn, it is believed that the silence or non-communicative behavior simply helps him avoid extremely high levels of discomfort and anxiety. The child is likely to be scared rather than angry or stubborn.

- Sometimes present questions in a multiple-choice format (e.g., "Would you rather play with Legos or Playdoh?"). If he/she does not answer, wait 5 seconds and ask the question again.

- Please be careful about describing the child as shy—this may seem like a kind response but it leads the child and others to believe that the behavior cannot change.

- Quietly praise the child and provide support when he uses forms of communication that involve reaching out and responding to others. Nonchalantly giving praise like "Thanks for letting me know" or "I'm glad you told me" is appropriate.

- Actively support the child's inclusion and ensure peers do not interpret silence as disinterest/rudeness.

Try to avoid:

- Guessing at what the child is telling you nonverbally. Spending a long time in nonverbal interactions may diminish the child's motivation for using words at a later time.

- Pressuring, bribing, threatening, flattering, or cajoling the child into speaking.

- Completely removing opportunities for children speak—if children do not have any opportunity or reason to speak, they probably will not speak.

SAMPLE SCHOOL LETTER

Letter Requesting Consideration of an Individualized Education Plan

Everything between brackets should be customized. Be sure to edit content in order to reflect your child's specific situation. Be sure to send a copy to the principal and/or school psychologist or counselor and keep a copy for yourself.

[Date]
[School]
[Address]
[City, State, Zip Code]

To Whom it May Concern,

My child, [child's name], is currently in [list program or grade] at [school name]. Given a recent diagnostic evaluation with [Dr's Name] and a subsequent diagnosis of selective mutism, a specific anxiety disorder, I would like to meet with the special education team to discuss [his/her] current placement situation and to look at how we can modify [his/her] current goals and objectives to better fit [his/her] educational needs.

(Edit this paragraph to reflect your specific situation: My child is regressing. [He/she] is not benefiting from [his/her] current placement. I am concerned that [he/she] is unable to participate in oral presentations and group projects. If [he/she] is injured, [he/she] may not be able to indicate that [he/she] needs help.)

Children with Selective mutism need specific intervention plans in the school setting, including working with a "keyworker"—someone in the school setting who can practice "being brave" and encouraging speech with (child's name). [Dr's name] is happy to assist in setting up an intervention plan with this keyworker, as well as helping to develop accommodations in the classroom.

Please schedule a meeting as soon as possible so that we can discuss these issues and consider an accommodations and/or intervention plan. I would prefer being contacted with time options in advance so that the meeting can be scheduled at a mutually agreeable time and place.

I look forward to hearing from you within the next five school days.

Sincerely,

[Parent/Guardian Name]
[Address]
[City, State, Zip Code]
[Phone Number]

SAMPLE SELECTIVE MUTISM INTERVENTION AND ACCOMMODATION PLAN RECOMMENDATIONS

(*Not all listed interventions and accommodations are appropriate for every child, thus, interventions should be chosen based on the needs of the child and developed in conjunction with the intervention team with the goal of meeting those needs.)

1. [Student] may benefit from working in individualized sessions with a "keyworker" (a school-based professional in charge of practicing "brave work" with the child, generalizing to all school environments, and communicating with other involved team members). These sessions should consist of behavioral interventions, using shaping and stimulus fading procedures to reduce the child's anxiety and increase communication at a slow, steady pace. More information about the development of an intervention plan within the school can be found in *Selective Mutism* by Aimee Kotrba, Ph.D. This intervention must begin one-on-one in a closed-office setting, and once speech has been obtained the child and keyworker can begin working in different settings and including an increasing number of individuals.

2. [Student] should at first be encouraged to increase communication and participate in the classroom and socially, even if that communication is nonverbal at first. Eventually, attempts should be made to reinforce and attend to only verbal language, so as to extinguish the use of nonverbal communication.

3. Allow [student] extra time to respond to questions. At least five seconds should be provided after every communication prompt or question, in order to all [student] an opportunity to answer.

4. Take care not to make too much direct eye contact, as this can increase [student's] anxiety.

5. [Student] should be given alternative ways of completing oral assignments if necessary, including written projects, audio/videotaping the child presenting at home, allowing a peer or the teacher to present the written work while the child points to a poster board, etc.

6. The classroom teacher will provide nonverbal assessments.

7. [Student] should never be punished and/or criticized, and should not receive reduced grades because of the lack of speech.

8. When the child does communicate, no extra attention or overt praise should be given to the child, as this might increase anxiety. Matter-of-fact praise (such as "Thanks for letting me know") can be given nonchalantly.

9. [Student] shall be permitted, if necessary, to take any standardized test outside of the regular classroom, either privately or in a small group, administered by the keyworker, in case [she/he] needs to ask a question or seek clarification.

10. Home/school communication will be available on a daily or weekly basis with both the classroom teacher and the "key worker." It is recommended that this communication take the form of a "Brave Work Log" (as seen in _____ by Aimee Kotrba, Ph.D.). Copies can be placed in a 3-ring binder and passed around to team members. All team members (e.g., teacher, keyworker, psychologist, parent) can record progress so as to maximize communication.

11. Assign [Student] a seat with a close friend on each side, close to the teacher, away from door.

12. Assign [Student Name] a seat at lunch next to friends.

13. Assign scheduled times for bathroom breaks. Have [Student] and [her/his] buddy accompany each other to the bathroom.

14. Prepare [Student] for changes in routine (e.g., substitute teachers) and special large group activities (e.g., substitutes, fire drills, schedule changes, field trips). All substitute teachers should be made aware of the child's accommodations.

15. All adults who come into contact with [Student] should be advised of the intervention plan (e.g., teacher, extras teachers, lunch personnel, office staff, etc.).

16. The classroom teacher may provide individual rapport-building time with [Student] and possibly a friend or two, before/after school or during lunch. This will allow [Student] extra time to build comfort, and thereby increase the likelihood of communication.

17. Allow [Student] to spend time with [her/his] teacher before the school year starts. This may take the form of working with the child and keyworker to transfer speech prior to the end of the previous school year, and/or may include coming into the school in the days prior to school beginning to get comfortable and develop rapport with the new teacher. The open-house is not adequate, since it is generally short, conducted in a group, and may be chaotic and anxiety-provoking for [Student]. Instead, these meetings should be only the teacher, child, and parent or keyworker, and should be done in a relaxed and fun manner.

18. Allow [Student]'s parents/family members to have access to the school environment during off hours (before and after school, during summer months) to promote comfort and eventually verbalization when alone with a parent and eventually, one or more peers or a teacher.

19. If the child is working with a clinical psychologist outside of the school setting, consider inviting the psychologist into the school for sessions in order to generalize "brave work" into the school setting. Minimally, the psychologist should be invited to participate in team meetings in the school.

20. Each year [Student] should be moved up to the next teacher with his/her close friends, particularly with those to whom he/she speaks. [Student] will be placed with accepting teachers to be chosen with team and parent input.

21. The district will provide faculty training through consultations and attendance at SM conferences. Appropriate workshops and seminars can be found at www.selectivemutism. org on the calendar of events.

22. The district will purchase selective mutism educational materials to educate the child's teachers and all school personnel. A training video for school professionals on treating selective mutism is available at www.selectivemutismtreatment.com.

23. The school will provide quarterly parent/faculty meetings to update and report upon accommodations and progress.

24. Resources on selective mutism should be utilized for further suggestions and information about [Student]'s condition. Please visit the Selective Mutism Group at www.selectivemutism.org for up-to-date information for teachers, professionals and parents. It is recommended that all individuals within the school who will be acting as interventionists (e.g., keyworkers, teachers, etc.) read *Selective Mutism* by Aimee Kotrba, Ph.D., in order to fully understand the conceptualization of Selective mutism as well as the details and workings of the intervention plan.

REFERENCES

For your convenience, you may download a PDF version of the Treatment Forms and Handouts in this book from our website: go.pesi.com/SelectiveMutism

American Psychiatric Association. (2013). *Diagnostic and statistical manual of mental disorders, 5th ed.* Arlington, VA: American Psychiatric Publishing.

American Speech-Language-Hearing Association. (n.d.). *Acquiring English as a Second Language.* Retrieved May 1, 2014, from http://www.asha.org/public/speech/development/easl.htm#sthash.MfUS4JQf.dpuf:

Barnett, D., Bauer, A., Bell, S., Elliott, N., Haski, H., Barkley, E., et al. (2007). Preschool Intervention Scripts: Lessons from 20 Years of Research and Practice. *The Journal of Speech-Language Pathology and Applied Behavior Analysis, 2,* 158-181.

Beidel, D.C. (1996). Assessment of childhood social phobia: Construct, convergent, and discriminative validity of the Social Phobia and Anxiety Inventory for Children (SPAI-C). *Psychological Assessment, 8*(3), 235-240.

Bergman R.L., Piacentini, J., McCracken, J.T. (2002). Prevalance and description of selective mutism in a school-based sample. *Journal of the American Academy of Child and Adolescent Psychiatry, 41*(8), 938-946.

Bergman, R.L., Gonzoles, A., Piacentini, J., (2013). Integrated Behavior Therapy for selective mutism: A randomized controlled pilot study. *Behaviour research and therapy, 51,* 680-689.

Blum, N., Kell, R., Starr, H., Lender, W., Bradley-Klug, K., Osborne, M., et al. (1998). Case study: audio feedforward treatment of selective mutism. *Journal of the American Academy of Child and Adolescent Psychiatry, 37*(1), 40-43.

Blumberg, S. B. (2013). Changes in parent-reported prevalence of autism spectrum disorder in school-aged US children: 2007 to 2011-2012. *National Health Statistics Reports, 65,* 1-12.

Chavira, D.A., Shipon-Blum, E., Stein, M.B. (2007). Selective mutism and social anxiety disorder: All in the family? *Journal of the American Academy of Child and Adolescent Psychiatry, 46*(11), 1464-1472.

Cohan, S.L., Chavira, D.A., Shipon-Blum, E., Hitchcock, C., Roesch, S.C., & Stein, M.B. (2008). Refining the classification of children with selective mutism: A latent profile analysis. *Journal of Clinical Child and Adolescent Psychology, 37*(4), 770-784.

Davis, M. (1992). The role of the amygdala in fear and anxiety. *Annual Review of Neuroscience, 15*(1), 353-375.

Dunn Buron, K. (2007). *A 5 Could Make Me Lose Control! An activity-based method for evaluating and supporting highly anxious students.* Lenexa: Autism Aspergers Publishing Company. Lenexa: KS.

Garcia, A.M. (2004). Selective mutism. In: *Phobic and Anxiety Disorders in Children and Adolescents: A Clinician's Guide to Psychosocial and Pharmacological Interventions* (pp. 433-456). New York: Oxford University Press.

Grice, K. (2002). Eligibility under IDEA for other health impaired children. *School Law Bulletin,* 8-12.

Head Start. (2006). *Policy and Regulations for Eligibility Criteria: Speech and Language Impairments.* Retrieved December 20, 2013, from Head Start: http://eclkc.ohs.acf.hhs.gov/hslc/standards/Head%20Start%20Requirements/1308/1308.9%20%20Eligibility%20criteria_%20Speech%20or%20language%20impairments..htm

Kearney, C.A. & Vecchio, J. (2006). Functional analysis and treatment of selective mutism in children. *Journal of Speech-Language Pathology and Applied Behavioral Analysis, 1*(2), 141-148.

Klein, E.R., Armstrong, S.L., Shipon-Blum, E. (2013). Assessing spoken language competence in children with selective mutism: Using parents as test presenters. *Communications Disorders Quarterly, 34*(3), 1-12.

Koeppen, A.S. (1974). Relaxation training for children. *Elementary School Guidance and Counseling, 9*(1), 14-21.

Krysanski, V.L. (2003). A brief review of selective mutism literature. *Journal of Psychology, 137*(1), 29-40.

Kumpulainen, K. (2002). Phenomonology and treatment of selective mutism. *CNS Drugs, 16*(3), 175-180.

Kurtz, S. (2011, October). Treating professional's guide to the functional behavioral assessment of selective mutism. *Presented at the Selective Mutism Group Conference.* New York, NY.

Kurtz, S. (2013, October). Intensive treatment of selective mutism. *Presented at the Selective Mutism Group Annual Conference.* Berkeley, CA.

Kussmaul, A. (1877). *Die Stoerungen der Sprache [Disturbances in linguistic function].* Basel, Switzerland: Benno Schwabe.

Lynas, C. (2012, October). I want to face my fears: how parents can promote change in their child with selective mutism. *Presented at the Selective Mutism Group Annual Conference.* Berkeley, CA.

Matzner, F. Silva, R., Silvan, M., Chowdhury M., Nastasi, L. (1997, May). Preliminary test-retest reliability of the KID-SCID. *Presented at the Scientific Proceedings of American Psychatric Association Meeting.* San Diego, CA.

McNeil, C. & Hembree-Kigin, T.L. (2011). *Parent-Child Interaction Therapy (Issues in Clinical Child Psychology).* New York:Springer.

Muchnik, C., Ari-Even Roth, D., Hildesheimer, M., Arie, M., Bar-Haim, Y., Henkin, Y. (2013). Abnormalities in auditory efferent activities in children with selective mutism. *Audiology and Neurotology, 18*(6), 353-361.

Oerbeck, B., Stein, M., Wentzel-Larsen, T., Langsrud, O., Kristensen, H. (2013). A randomized controlled trial of a home and school-based intervention for selective mutism—defocused communicaiton and behavioural techniques. *Child and Adolescent Mental Health.* DOI; 10.1111/camh.12045.

Pearson Education. (n.d.). *Pearsons: Clinical Assessment.* Retrieved July 17, 2012, from Pearsons Website: http://www.pearsonassessments.com/HAIWEB/Cultures/en-us/Productdetail.htm?Pid=0158036603

Pionek Stone, B., Kratochwill, T., Sladezcek, I., Serlin, D.C. (2002). Treatment of selective mutism: A best-evidence synthesis. *School Psychology Quarterly, 17*(2), 168-190.

Reynolds, C.R., Kamphaus, R.W. (2004). *BASC-2: Behavior assessment system for children, second edition manual.* Circle Pines, MN: AGS Publishing.

Rohrer, D., Taylor, K., Pashler, H., Cepeda, N.J., Wixted, J.T. (2005). The effect of overlearning on long-term retention. *Applied Cognitive Psychology, 19*, 361-374.

Rollnick, S. & Miller, W.R. (1995). What is motivational interviewing? *Behavioural and Cognitive Psychotherapy, 23*, 325-334.

Schill, M.T., Kratochwill, T.R., Gardner, W.I. (1996). An assessment protocol for selective mutism: Analogue assessment using parents as facilitators. *Journal of School Psychology, 34*(1), 1-21.

Schultz, E. (2014, April). Program Evaluation of Group Therapy for selective mutism. *Masters Thesis Defense.* Dearborn, MI, USA: University of Michigan–Dearborn.

Schwartz, R.H., Freedy, A.S., Sheridan, M.J. (2006). Selective mutism: Are primary care physicians missing the silence? *Clinical Pediatrics, 45*(1), 43-48.

Sharoni, M. (2012). Selective mutism. *The Israeli Journal of Pediatrics, 79*, 18-21.

Shipon-Blum, E. (2003). *The ideal classroom setting for the selectively mute child.* Philadelphia, PA: SMart Center Publications.

Shriver, M.D., Segool, N., Gortmaker, V. (2011). Behavior Observations for Linking Assessment to Treatment of selective mutism. *Education and Treatment of Children, 34*(3), 389-411.

Steinhausen, H.C., Wachter, M., Laimbock, K., Metzke, C.W. (2005). A long-term outcome study of selective mutism in childhood. *Journal of Child Psychology and Psychiatry, 47*(7), 751-756.

Vecchio, J., Kearney, C.A. (2009). Treating youths with selective mutism with an alternating design of exposure-based practice and contingency management. *Behavior Therapy, 40*(4), 380-392.

Yeganeh, R., Beidel, D.C., Turner, S.M., Pina, A.A., Silverman, W.K. (2003). Clinical distinctions between selective mutism and social phobia: An investigation of childhood psychopathology. *Journal of the American Academy of Child and Adolescent Psychiatry, 42*(9), 1069-1075.

Author Biography

Aimee Kotrba, Ph.D, is a licensed clinical psychologist specializing in the expert assessment and treatment of Selective Mutism and Social Anxiety. Dr. Kotrba is the owner and lead psychologist at Thriving Minds Behavioral Clinic in Brighton, Michigan, a specialty clinic dedicated to effective treatment for children with Selective Mutism and other pediatric anxiety disorders.

Dr. Kotrba currently serves as the president of the Selective Mutism Group (SMG) Board of Directors and as the psychological expert for a local Selective Mutism parent support group. Her work has appeared in numerous media outlets, including *Livingston County Parent Journal* and *MetroParent Magazine*. She is a nationally recognized speaker and regularly offers local, national, and international workshops on the identification and treatment of Selective Mutism for parents, professionals, and school personnel.

Made in the USA
Middletown, DE
13 June 2015